A CONTINUING MARVEL

The Story of

The Museum of Science and Industry

Major Lenox R. Lohr, president of the Museum of Science & Industry from 1940 to 1968.

A CONTINUING MARVEL

*The Story of
The Museum of Science
and Industry*

by Herman Kogan

1973
DOUBLEDAY & COMPANY, INC., GARDEN CITY, NEW YORK

Color photographs courtesy of
The Museum of Science and Industry

ISBN: 0-385-02259-X
Library of Congress Catalog Card Number 72–92405
Copyright © 1973 by Herman Kogan
First Edition

CONTENTS

A CONTINUING MARVEL
The Story of
The Museum of Science and Industry

CHAPTER I

"A MOST SERVICEABLE
INSTITUTION . . ."

The Museum of Science and Industry sits in regal dignity off
Chicago's southern shore of Lake Michigan. Its exterior is
stately and ornate, but beyond its massive bronze doors and
past the great portico, motion and action abound, the halls
are filled with the constant hum of voices and the buzz
of excitement, and everywhere there are light and sound.

In this remarkable place, on every day of the year except
Christmas, a visitor can create a rock fault or a rainfall or
an electrical storm, see chicks and ducklings emerging into
life through their fragile eggshells, test for color blindness
or automobile-driving skills or the condition of heart, ears,
or lungs. He can descend into a coal mine and ride its pit
cars past miners working the face of a vein, hear his voice as
it sounds on a telephone and see its wavy pulsations on an
oscilloscope, work the controls of a submarine and peer
through its periscope, move a forty-eight-hundred-pound
bearing with a fingertip, observe lights arranged to re-
create human cellular movement. He can stroll through a
fully equipped farm or from aorta to ventricle in the interior of a throbbing, fourteen-foot model of the human
heart or through the chambers of a twenty-four-foot reproduction of a human cell enlarged a million times, pedal a
stationary bicycle to generate energy for a light bulb, shoot

anti-toxin into a simulated arm with a pressure gun or operate an artificial limb, grow nostalgic over the earliest of Mary Pickford's movies, or reflect on present and future uses of the revolutionary laser beam. And more.

Little wonder that this institution—perhaps the world's largest devoted to informal, mass education on the principle that learning can be fun—is most often called "The Liveliest Show in Town" and "The Educational Playhouse" and is, by all odds, the area's prime tourist attraction, with an annual attendance mark of over three million.

More than the fact that no admission is charged is responsible for that impressive attendance statistic. For this is truly a "people's museum." Except for a gentle reminder on its exterior during the summer months, PLEASE DO NOT ENTER IN BATHING ATTIRE, nowhere are there any signs demanding "Silence" or admonishing "Hands Off" or "Do Not Touch." Visitors are invited and encouraged to become involved and to participate in everything that surrounds them in the fourteen acres of exhibits spread over three floors. There are levers to tug, buttons to push, cranks to turn, dials to twirl. Whistles blast. Wheels spin. Machines thump. Colored lights flash.

Each morning, half an hour or more before the doors are swung open to welcome visitors, department heads, staff members, and guide-lecturers gather—some at a conference table and the rest in another room—to listen to a recorded rundown on the upcoming day's special activities, notable guests, anticipated number of student tours. An out-of-order memo is distributed to those responsible for the Museum's maintenance, with the unwritten but urgently understood proviso that any defect in the Museum's vast array of mechanical, electronic, hydraulic, and audio-visual devices —fifteen hundred motors, sixty-six motion-picture projectors, 142 tape-playing machines feeding information into 375 hand sets, seventy-two slide projectors—must be repaired as soon as possible. So meticulous is the housekeeping

that brass trimmings are polished every morning and walls
scrubbed clean of every blemish.

Hardly a morning begins without a procession of large,
orange-hued buses rolling into the parking lot north of the
Museum. Crowds of school children emerge, lunch bags
clutched in their hands to be deposited in large wicker baskets inside the entrance for later distribution in one of eight
dining rooms. Hour after hour, family groups embark from
automobiles, children inevitably leading the way to the
handsome building. Before a typical day ends, those who
have walked up the broad stairway past the sign about the
bathing attire and another that reads ARE YOUR CAR LIGHTS
TURNED OFF? will invariably include foreign visitors speaking
in many tongues—Russian, French, German, Japanese, Ital-
ian, Spanish—and scores of others from communities all
over the United States. Their average stay, reckoned by
surveys, is three hours and twelve minutes, a visiting period
of considerable length, but quite obviously far short of the
time needed to see all or a substantial portion of the Museum's attractions.

To encompass what the Museum has to offer, visitors must
return again and again—and vast numbers do—to make their
way through hundreds of exhibits whose total worth is fifty
million dollars and whose fascinating and instructive machines and contrivances constitute a vivid array of scientific
and industrial accomplishments.

2.

The building in which these wondrous things are housed
had risen in all its classic splendor after an energetic group
of Chicagoans, having wrested from other cities the privilege
of celebrating formally the four-hundredth anniversary of
Columbus' discovery of America, created the World's Columbian Exposition of 1893.

Augustus Saint-Gaudens, then America's foremost sculptor, praised it as "unequaled since the Parthenon and the age of Pericles," though mindful of the vast array of other structures that would transform the windswept sandy ridges and marshes of Jackson Park into what one architectural historian later acclaimed "a spectacle unequaled in the history of the world for the magnificence of its beauty." Indeed, it was Saint-Gaudens who had first proposed to Daniel H. Burnham, the Chicago architect in charge of all construction, the need for a structure in which to contain the masses of paintings and sculpture that would be heading toward the city from all over the world. "Look here, old fellow," he told Burnham at one of the innumerable planning sessions in 1891, "do you realize that this fair has brought together the greatest meeting of artists that has occurred since the fifteenth century?"

Burnham agreed. John Wellborn Root, his chief designer, had died suddenly, so he looked toward the East and chose Charles B. Atwood, an architect who had designed mansions for the Vanderbilt family in New York, had won top honors for his enlargement of New York's City Hall, and was steeped in Greek architectural forms and archaeology. Atwood, an imposingly handsome man, was ultimately responsible in large and small degree for designing some sixty buildings at the exposition, but it was on this one—variously called the Palace of Fine Arts and the Fine Arts Building— that he spent most of his time and lavished most of his attention, supplementing his own ideas with those of a French architect, Albert Besnard, with whom he had studied at the École des Beaux Arts.

The result was a magnificent structure costing seven hundred thousand dollars, severely classic in Ionic style, with a main pavilion and two flanking annexes covering six and a half acres and fronted by a lagoon on the south and a verdant lawn and an assortment of smaller, state buildings on the north. Its central dome, capped by a colossal reproduction of the Winged Victory, rose 125 feet, and its exterior ornamental moldings were modeled on those adorning the Erechtheum, one of the temples on the Athenian Acropolis, with its twenty-four caryatids, or supporting columns sculptured in the forms of women, on the façade designed by Saint-Gaudens himself.

Some exposition officials had qualms about whether European art museums and collectors would deign to contribute works, because Chicago was still famed more for its raucous ways than for its devotion to the nobler arts and believed to be too distant from New York, then deemed the center of culture and education in the United States. But the fears proved groundless. No sooner were invitations received from the State Department than applications for wall space started to arrive from countries everywhere. To the gratification of the exposition managers and Halsey C. Ives, chief of the art department, who had toured Europe's important art centers for six months during 1892 on a promotional mission, allotments for space requested by Great Britain, France, Germany, Austria, Italy, Belgium, Switzerland, Russia, Japan, Sweden, Norway, Denmark, and South American countries exceeded the total at the Paris Exposition of 1889. When the Palace of Fine Arts opened its stately doors, over ten thousand works on display in its seventy-four separate galleries ranged from characteristic "peasant pictures" of Millet and landscapes of Constable to creations of such Impressionists as Monet and Pissarro, of which a local critic wrote, "Although they affect the uninitiated with a sense of rawness and incompleteness, they are nevertheless to be regarded with interest, if not with mixed admiration." Characteristically, the American art collection was the largest, with close to two thousand pieces, which included contributions from such local notables as Charles Tyson Yerkes, the traction magnate and sometime corrupter of city and state legislators; Potter Palmer, the merchant/hotel owner whose regally styled wife, Bertha, was president of the fair's board of lady managers; and Martin A. Ryerson of the steelmaking family.

For all their grandeur, none of the structures on the fair's seven hundred acres was meant to be permanent, constructed mostly of "staff," a mixture of plaster and fiber. The Palace of Fine Arts was another matter, a fact due not so much to any original intention of Burnham's or Atwood's but to the insistence of several of the contributing countries that it be fireproofed before their paintings and sculpture were sent to the exposition. Consequently the fair managers revised their original plans. All the walls and inner partitions, resting on solid brick and concrete foundations, were lined with two or three feet of bricks (thirteen million were used for the entire building), and the roofs were supported by iron columns and steel trusses. And when a fire swept the grounds in February 1894, after the exposition's end, the Palace of Fine Arts stood foremost among the few survivors as a relic of the glory that had been Chicago's in that resplendent summer of 1893.

3.

When the Palace of Fine Arts was going up, Burnham had marveled at it and declared, "Some day it will be made permanent in stone," and from other quarters had come similar sentiments, ebulliently exemplified in one of many souvenir books of photographs: "Of all the buildings of the White City, this is one which art-lovers have desired to preserve, and if it were possible to convert it into enduring marble it would certainly be the brightest jewel of American architectural skill—a hope which is still cherished by thousands whom it has already delighted."

The year following the great 1893 exposition was hardly the time for carrying out such an ambitious notion, for depression and labor strife scourged the land. Yet the Palace

of Fine Arts was not left vacant. At the urging of Edward
E. Ayer—whose fascinating collection of North American Indian apparel, artifacts, and other materials had been exhibited at the exposition—Marshall Field, the city's prime
merchant, gave a million dollars toward the establishment
there of a natural history museum. Into the building, in
1894, went maps and writings of cartographers of Columbus'
era, a rusted anchor from one of the explorer's ships, and the
doors of the house he occupied at Porto Santo in the Madeira
Islands, and, from other exposition collections, the largest
group of meteorites then extant, botanical specimens, a
variety of birds of North and South America, representative
clothes of American Indians and Eskimos, and jewels both
genuine and in replica.

The name now affixed to the building was the Field Columbian Museum, and for the next twenty-six years it flourished as such. In 1905 the name was changed to the Field
Museum of Natural History; the area was continually en-
dowed with additional exhibits, including stuffed animals
from several hunting expeditions led by Theodore Roosevelt.
While thus occupied, the building was kept in steady repair. But by mid-1920 the Field Museum of Natural History
climaxed a five-year plan by moving northward to a gleaming white Georgian marble structure on the edge of Grant
Park. Deterioration of the abandoned building began
swiftly, lake winds and ice and sleet combining to chip
away at the wood-and-plaster exterior.

Almost at once, agitation developed not only for salvaging
the edifice but for restoring it to its former glory. Foremost
among the campaigners were the members of the local chapter of the American Institute of Architects, whose president, George W. Maher, acclaimed the building as "the
last remaining memorial of a great architectural achievement" and emphasized that despite its decaying exterior appearance, its walls were sound and solid and all its structural
features were still in good condition. In a widely distributed

booklet, *A Challenge to Civic Pride*, the architects made persuasive arguments, citing the building's history, its place in world architecture, its possible uses, and its public value: "Do you know that it can be restored in permanent form for $2,000,000 and made ready for use, but would cost $12,000,-000 if built new? Therefore to permit it to become a ruin by inaction is a public extravagance." A local bard, Wilbur D. Nesbit, composed a poem for the booklet, its concluding lines reading:

> "The hand of man should ever leave it free
> Save to make whole the finger-touch of Time,
> So that the children of the years to be
> May know, with us, the beauty still sublime."

Not everyone in the profession agreed. Andrew N. Rebori, a brilliant architect and determinedly inconoclastic, led the scoffers, asserting that the building had already served its purpose and had been reduced to "a scaly wormy pile that should be allowed to die." In the *Architectural Record* he wrote, "Let's make a fine scale model of the Fine Arts Building and put it in a shrine for coming generations instead of patching up the old ruin. Let's quit being a lot of sentimental idiots and grow up!"

But the ranks of supporters grew. Lorado Taft, the distinguished sculptor, added his plea to those of the architects and diverse organizations ranging from the Union League Club and the Chicago Association of Commerce to the Committee of One Hundred, an aggregation of civic boosters headed by Colonel William Nelson Pelouze, brother-in-law of the city's flamboyant mayor, William Hale "Big Bill" Thompson. Taft's ambition was to use the central pavilion of the restored building as a branch of the Art Institute of Chicago, as a museum of sculpture that would trace the development of this art form through the ages. Other advocates of restoration proposed such diverse uses as a community and recreational art center, a home for the practice of all the creative arts, including music and drama, an industrial art school, a huge convention hall. The Illinois Federation of Women's Clubs sparked a drive to raise funds for refurbishing at least one corner of building to prove that restoration was feasible, to emphasize the architectural beauty of the structure, and to stimulate public interest and support; by 1922 some seven thousand dollars was gathered for this purpose, and a process using quartz, Portland cement, and reinforced concrete gave the restored corner a rich, old-marble effect.

By this time, the five-man South Park Board, having earlier taken a three-to-two vote to demolish the building, was being importuned to reverse itself by Colonel Robert R. McCormick in editorials in his powerful Chicago *Tribune* and in personal messages to Edward J. Kelly, the rising Democratic politician who, with John Bain, a prominent banker, had voted against demolition. "We just can't afford to let this building go," read one letter. "Once restored, its beauty will be an inspiration to travelers from all over our country, just as it was to visitors to the fair. . . . To vote its destruction is a shame. As to the use to which the restored building can be put, he assured that some use will be found, and it will be a noble one." In a typical editorial, commenting on proposals to spend fifteen million dollars on improvements along Lake Michigan, the *Tribune* proposed that at least a million dollars be applied to the restoration. "To ignore this asset while spending millions on more drives and more grass plots would be not only stupidity from the practical point of view but a sad confession of lack of feeling for the rare achievements of creative genius. The Fine Arts Building is supreme and unique. . . ." Kelly managed to stall final action on the demolition decision until a new member, Bernard E. Sunny of the Illinois Bell Telephone

Company, joined the board; he promptly ranged himself alongside Kelly and Bain, thereby preventing, for the time being, any move to tear down the building.

4.

All this activity and these rosy predictions might well have gone for naught were it not for a Chicagoan whose earnest philanthropy in a variety of areas had already made him one of the city's—and, indeed, the nation's—major benefactors. Obviously aware of the various campaigns swirling around the fate of the old Palace of Fine Arts, Julius Rosenwald, head of Sears Roebuck and Co., broached a plan in November 1921 to Samuel Insull, then president of the influential Commercial Club of Chicago. "I have long felt," wrote Rosenwald, "that Chicago should have as one of its most important institutions for public usefulness a great Industrial Museum or Exhibition, in which might be housed, for permanent display, machinery and working models illustrative of as many as possible of the mechanical processes of production and of manufacture." Noting that such a place was indigenous to Chicago and that exhibits of this kind invariably drew large crowds at various exposi-tions and fairs, Rosenwald spelled out the advantages that would accrue to the city: "In an industrial center like Chicago there ought to be a permanent exhibit of this charac-ter, for the entertainment and instruction of the people; a place where workers in technical trades, students, engineers and scientists might have opportunity to enlarge their vi-sion; to gain better understanding of their own problems by contact with actual machinery, and by quiet examination in leisure hours of working models of apparatus; or, perhaps, to make new contributions to the world's welfare through helpful inventions. The stimulating influence of such an exhibit upon the growing youth of the city needs only to be mentioned."

The notion of establishing such an institution had absorbed Rosenwald for at least a decade. He had first been stimulated toward his thinking during a visit with members of his family to Munich in 1911. There, his eight-year-old son, William, had discovered and been fascinated by trips to a unique museum in the old barracks of the Bavarian National Museum on Maximilianstrasse, where, in contrast to the decorously dull tours the family made in the famous Alte Pinakothek, one of Munich's art galleries, there was action and excitement. By pushing buttons or working levers or dropping a coin in a slot, William could generate static electricity, see pistons traveling back and forth in engines whose cylinders had been cut open, light up an X-ray machine so that the bones in his hand were strikingly revealed when held up against a fluorescent screen, and look at the wheels of a jacked-up steam locomotive spin around. Instead of stern guards in stiff uniforms commanding silence, affable attendants answered questions, however naive, and encouraged visitors to work the marvelous machines and ingenious devices.

This distinctive establishment bore the unwieldy official title of The German Museum for the Preservation of the Mysterious Past in Natural Science and History of Engineering but was famous throughout Europe as the Deutsches Museum. It had been founded in 1903 by Oskar von Miller, foremost among German electrical engineers, on the principle that in addition to preserving masterpieces of engineering and science—as had been done for years in such older technical museums as the Science Museum of South Kensington in London and the Conservatoire des Arts et Métiers in Paris—scientific history could be delineated and technology more vividly taught with the aid of sectioned models that, with the push of a button or the turn of a crank, could show how industry's devices large and small were developed and how they worked. In exhibit after exhibit, which constituted a literal "museum in motion," functioning apparatus and devices traced the step-by-step progress of man's endeavors from primeval days to counterparts in the modern era. To allow visitors to participate in the actual operation of such machines was quite radical when Dr. von Miller proposed it to German industrialists whose financial support was required. But they accepted without hesitation his idea for a museum that would be considerably more than the usual repository of historical models. Under his direction and with application of his expertise in electrical engineering, the Deutsches Museum had rapidly become a tourist attraction as heavily patronized as Munich's art galleries, opera house, theaters and palaces and innumerable beer halls.

His son's buoyant enthusiasm drew Rosenwald to the museum, and an instructive meeting with the director. Von Miller took the philanthropist on a special tour and informed him that in that very year an isle in the Isar River, running through the heart of the city, was being set aside for construction of a large and comprehensive set of buildings to house his ever-expanding enterprise. On subsequent trips to the city, Rosenwald rarely failed to meet with von Miller to be kept informed of the progress—or lack of it, especially during the World War I years—in moving and installing close to fifty thousand objects in the newly built museum.

Rosenwald's letter to Insull contained more than a suggestion for a similar museum in Chicago which would be the first of its kind in the country. As ever, he was prepared to offer financial support for a permanent exhibition that "might become a most serviceable institution for the people and a radiating influence for notable industrial progress." If his proposal met with the approval of the Commercial Club and the enterprise was undertaken under its guidance and auspices, concluded Rosenwald, "I am prepared to make a very substantial contribution, under certain conditions to be agreed upon, toward the fund needed to assure the establishment and maintenance of such a permanent Industrial Museum." That very substantial contribution, he assured Insull, would be one million dollars.

CHAPTER II

JULIUS ROSENWALD'S GIFT

When Julius Rosenwald made his initial offer, he included no mention of any possibility that the fine old ruin in Jackson Park might be suitable for the intended purpose. In fact, although he expressed deep appreciation for cultural contributions to the city by the Art Institute and the Field Museum of Natural History, he indicated that a building "perhaps practical in type rather than monumental" was needed to bring "even greater gain to the masses of people of our city because of its more intimate relationship to the practical affairs of daily life." Yet he was soon persuaded, while consideration of his proposal languished and as the ranks of proponents of rehabilitation swelled and public clamor grew louder, to consider the Palace of Fine Arts as a logical site. A few months later Rosenwald offered to pay half the cost of restoring the building if the other half could be appropriated by the Board of South Park Commissioners, but no action was taken.

By April 1924 the various campaigns and public opinion had crystallized behind a suggestion that a bond issue of five million dollars be approved for submission to voters, its purpose being primarily to reconstruct the building for a huge municipal convention hall, combined with an industrial museum, a school of industrial arts, a Women's Memorial Hall, a complex of centers devoted to athletics, art, and social activities, and a museum of architecture and sculpture. Edward J. Kelly was now the board's president; he urged passage of the bond issue, designating Ernest R. Graham, who had worked as a young man with Atwood and whose architects' firm had created the new Field Museum of Natural History, as the man to devise what an editorialist for the Chicago *Herald and Examiner* predicted would be "the greatest edifice since Rome's Colosseum."

After voters sanctioned the bond issue, Rosenwald still held to his theory that the building should be used entirely for an industrial museum instead of what he envisaged as a hodgepodge of assorted halls designed, as one supporter put it, "for civic betterment." He conferred often on the matter with his bright attorney and adviser, Leo F. Wormser, and with his associates at the Commercial Club. On December 11, 1925, Rosenwald and Wormser met with the club's president, doughty Sewell L. Avery, then head of the U. S. Gypsum Company, and such members as Colonel A. A. Sprague, the city's commissioner of public works, Charles Piez, president of the Link Belt Company, and Frank Wetmore, chairman of the First National Bank of Chicago, to discuss his ambitions for the industrial museum. Rosenwald was prepared, he told them, to subscribe no less than three million dollars for the establishment of such a museum, wherever the site. The Palace of Fine Arts he considered quite suitable, and he urged that informal conferences be held with Kelly and other South Park commissioners with a view toward persuading them to his point of view. The proposal, Rosenwald was assured, would be brought up before the club's executive committee and given every consideration, and at a subsequent meeting an Industrial Museum committee was organized, with Wetmore as its chairman.

Before this group could make decisions and recommendations, Rosenwald was off to Europe with William, now twenty-three, and Wormser, whose persuasive skills he

wanted in order to augment exhaustive inspections of the
Vienna Technical Museum and the Deutsches Museum.
The latter was finally in its new quarters with an immense
collection of exhibits, most popular of which was a completely equipped coal mine.

In Vienna, Rosenwald was interviewed by the Chicago
Tribune's famous correspondent Floyd Gibbons, who wrote
that although plans for the opening in Chicago of "the
greatest technical and industrial museum in the world"
were not yet complete, the "idea for the new institution has
assumed such a form in the mind of the philanthropist that
he discussed the proposition with undisguised enthusiasm."
Rosenwald emphasized in his talk with Gibbons the values
inherent for American youth. "Show him working models
of the earliest and latest harvesting and threshing machines
and the development of flour mills and the curious growth
of yeast and the workings of breadmaking machines and
you prove something through his own eyes. In such a museum young Chicago will be able to experience the thrills
of going down into the bowels of the earth and seeing how
coal is mined. How many non-technical people in Chicago
know why their voice carries over the telephone or why the
red-hot wires in a glass bottle make electric light or just
exactly what an air wave or magnetic field looks like?"

In Munich, Wormser arranged for photographers to take
motion pictures of the famous museum and thousands of
photographs of its exhibits, and in Paris, on their way home,
John Gunther of the Chicago *Daily News* snared both
men for still another interview, in which they not only
spoke of their ambitions for Chicago but reiterated the wonders of the new Deutsches Museum. "We saw cross-section exhibits of mines of all kinds, of canal construction, of
the applied mechanics of airplanes and dirigibles, of submarines and battleships," Rosenwald told Gunther. "We
saw not only models but the machines themselves—airplanes,
derricks, blast furnaces and all sorts of devices for metal-

lurgy, physics, chemistry and geology. Such exhibits, present without number in Munich, are the rightful heritage of any growing generation. They could be of great value in America for the interest and instruction of students and citizens." And from William came an echo of the wonderment of his boyhood visits years back. "One walks through entire life-size mines of all sorts containing machinery run by the attendants," he wrote to a friend. "They have an automatic screw-machine which manufactures tiny souvenir brass kegs. In the basement, they have the U-1, a submarine, completely cross-sectioned, also entire rooms as they would be in a model ship. . . . The apparatus is always so designed that the visitor may use it himself."

2.

So avid was the interest in negotiations for the museum that the interviews with Gibbons and Gunther were considered front-page news. But this was scant coverage compared with what ensued when, on August 17, 1926, formal announcement was made of Rosenwald's gift.

"VAST NEW MUSEUM FOR CITY," read the *Tribune*'s headline. Its story and others in all the newspapers stressed that Rosenwald's gift of three million dollars, announced at a luncheon in the Union League Club, would speed to reality the erection of the industrial museum so long discussed and wrangled over. Avery, reflecting on his own tours of the Deutsches Museum, declared, "It is education in a new form. And to know how it seizes the interest you must see it. Never a moment of boredom, nor a hint of the tedium that often comes with book learning does one experience." Chairman Kelly affirmed that he saw no obstacles to proceeding with the work ahead. A test suit brought by a lawyer, William E. Furlong, attacking the validity of the bond issue, had been rejected by the Illinois Supreme Court

the preceding April. Outside the crumbling building Kelly dutifully posed shaking hands with Rosenwald; both men were flanked by Wormser, Commissioner Michael L. Igoe, Avery, George T. Donoghue, general superintendent of the South Park Board, and two representatives of the Deutsches Museum, Dr. Albert Koch, second in command to Dr. von Miller, and Dr. Johann Biberg. After the picture-taking, Rosenwald left for the summer White House in up-state New York to confer with President Coolidge on business conditions and to inform him in detail about the projected museum.

Other reactions were immediate and unanimously favorable. E. N. Hurley, chairman of a commission arranging a vast lakefront fair to be held in 1933 to mark the city's one hundredth birthday, said that his plans had been given new impetus. Mayor William E. Dever, welcoming relief from incessant newspaper accounts of gang warfare and liquor hijackings, wrote a letter of appreciation to Rosenwald ("Splendid public spirited proposal . . . great value of your generosity"), as did Dr. Max Mason, president of the University of Chicago, F. E. Morrow, president of the Western Society of Engineers, and other dignitaries. At Rosenwald's and Wormser's assurances that the exterior of the building would be preserved in its entirety in accord with plans drawn by Ernest Graham's firm, Rufus C. Dawes, a business and civic leader who would later play a vital role in the development of the museum, intoned, "Mr. Rosenwald's generosity is matched only by his discrimination." Harold L. Ickes, then prominent in Chicago social reform movements, wrote Rosenwald, "I just want to say, apropos of your latest public-spirited act, that if Chicago has any finer citizen than yourself, I don't know who he is."

Editorialists in all the papers called on their most buoyant prose. To those who complained that the Palace of Fine Arts was too delicate in feeling for an industrial museum, the *Tribune* responded, "We do not accept this view. We believe

that modern technology is not the enemy of beauty but can be its servant. Housing an industrial museum in the midst of classic refinement impresses us as a recognition of the fact that the machine has brought leisure and with leisure a greater opportunity for the cultivation of beauty than the world has ever known." And in the *Daily News:* "Mr. Rosenwald's gift exemplifies sound judgment and discrimination. . . . Exhibits will be furnished from every direction and in a comparatively short time the famous Munich museum should have an American rival worthy of its highest standards." "We are on the threshold of a renaissance of industry under the impulse of the constructive arts bred in America," stated the Chicago *Evening Post.* In New York, the *Times* took note of the occasion with an editorial headed, "Chicago Doing It First" and lamented that city's laggard policy in setting up its industrial museum: "We have been 'saying' the thing so long that when we come to doing it, it should be better done for the waiting. Meanwhile, Chicago is to be congratulated on doing it first for America, and Mr. Rosenwald on having the vision, the disposition and the means to make it possible."

Edward A. Filene, the Boston philanthropist and department-store magnate, not only praised the project as basically important to Chicago's welfare but cited an added advantage: "It will show the youth of today the debt he owes to his forefathers. Our young people take all for granted—the radio, the telephone, the airplane. They overlook the self-abnegation, the martyrdom, the sacrifices that made these inventions possible." In Paris, Lorado Taft told John Gunther that while he was delighted with Rosenwald's action, he hoped that a portion of the restored museum might be used, as he said he had been assured by Kelly it would, for displaying a group of sculptural casts that would be of value to art students as well as to industrial students: "In proper surroundings, these arts can be made thrilling to responsive youth quite as much as a submarine or a dynamo. Michel-

angelo means more to some children than a submarine." On a visit to Chicago, the electrical wizard Michael Pupin lauded Rosenwald's action as "an inspiration to youth." And lesser-known citizens added their sentiments; typical was a Victor Cofman, writing in the *Tribune*'s "Voice of the People" column that it was a pleasant surprise to see headlines about a "vast museum" in place of the latest bulletins on the state of health of the ailing movie star Rudolph Valentino, and an A. M. Krensky, exuberant over Rosenwald's latest benefaction, suggested to the Chicago city council: "It would be especially fitting that the name of his own street where he has resided for so many years be changed from Ellis avenue to Rosenwald avenue."

3.

In the aftermath of the announcements and civic enthusiasm, various formalities were required.

The initial board of trustees, reflecting the industrial and business elite, came from the ranks of the Commercial Club. Besides Rosenwald, Wormser, Avery, Dawes, Sprague, Wetmore, and Piez, the members were William Rufus Abbott, president of the Illinois Bell Telephone Company; Edward F. Carry, president of The Pullman Company; Thomas E. Donnelley, president of R. R. Donnelley and Sons Company; John V. Farwell, director of the National Bank of the Republic; Robert P. Lamont, president of American Steel Foundries; Charles H. Markham, chairman of the Illinois Central Railroad; Theodore W. Robinson, vice-president of the Illinois Steel Company; Joseph T. Ryerson, president of Jos. T. Ryerson and Son; Robert W. Stewart, chairman of the Standard Oil Company of Indiana; Harold H. Swift, vice-president of Swift & Company; and Charles H. Thorne, retired chairman of Montgomery Ward & Co.

On September 14, 1926, the trustees met to authorize incorporation of the institution "not for pecuniary profit" and to affix a name to it. Earlier that month, Wormser had written to Rosenwald in New York that Avery insisted on calling it the Rosenwald Industrial Museum and that the trustees approved. By telegram, Rosenwald responded, "Museum of Science and Industry my preference. Cheerfully defer to majority opinions." Acting on this authority, the board applied for a charter in the name of the Rosenwald Industrial Museum. Then Rosenwald wired Wormser, "I appreciate more than I can tell the attitude of the committee, but after full, mature deliberation, I have decided that my name be omitted from the Museum title and that it be The Industrial Museum of Chicago. If I were contributing the building it might be a different matter but as that is the greater part of the investment it looks as though I was getting a bargain. Please therefore make this change before the matter goes any further."

Wormser replied that the application for the museum charter had already been filed in Springfield, and added, "But the committee after hearing your telegraphic views stated that it would have disregarded your protest even if telegram had come sooner. Everyone here feels this recognition due you for your many other meritorious acts regardless of recent Museum contribution." And the board itself was adamant in using Rosenwald's name "as a tribute to his munificence and citizenship."

Before the week was out, Rosenwald again wrote to Wormser: "Greatly as I appreciate the attitude of the Trustees, for whom I have the profoundest respect and for many of them real affection, I must insist upon the removal of my name. I am sure it is in the best interests of the project. If I were not convinced that it will in the long run be prejudicial, I would have been delighted to have my name connected with it, as you can readily imagine. If no name is used, it will belong to the people the same as the Art Institute. The people supply the building and will be taxed to support it and others will be solicited to give exhibits and again others to contribute money for memberships and special purposes. . . . Please therefore make it as easy as you can and see that the change is made. *The sooner the better.*" Wormser assented, but suggested delaying such a change, for he was deeply concerned with other activities crucial to the development of the project.

To intensify their interest further, Rosenwald paid the full expenses of a trip that Kelly and two of his fellow commissioners, John Bain and Louis J. Behan, and George T. Donoghue, and their wives, made to Europe early in 1927. In a two months' tour of London, Rome, Paris, Berlin, Vienna, and, of course, Munich, they inspected museums and parks, boulevards and sewage systems. After visiting the Deutsches Museum, Kelly told the *Daily News*'s Edgar Ansel Mowrer, "A museum in Chicago like this one would have the value of at least two years of education to persons who used it properly. The best thing about it is what it will do for the boys. I grew up in the stockyards district and I know what it would have meant to me and other boys if we had been able to get the inspiration of a great industrial museum."

On his return, Kelly was greeted at the La Salle Street Station by city officials and Democratic politicians and offered traditional comment: "Wonderful is the best word Mrs. Kelly and I had for our trip, but Chicago sure looks better to me this morning than the rest of the world." He also hinted that more funds than would be available from the sale of five million dollars in bonds might be needed to produce the kind of museum to rival the Deutsches Museum. "We will have to talk over the whole matter and come to some new estimates."

Wormser moved quickly in response to Kelly's statement about "new estimates." In a number of discussions with Kelly and the other commissioners, he won their agreement that the refurbished building would be used wholly for an industrial museum, adding that Rosenwald was prepared to give five hundred thousand dollars toward the erection of a civic convention hall elsewhere. To ease worries about additional costs of restoration, he added a significant clause to the formal contract with the South Park Board specifying that although Rosenwald had intended that his three million dollars be used primarily for maintaining, equipping, and operating the museum, up to a million dollars of this amount would be readily available if the reconstruction costs exceeded five million dollars. Also strengthened, so that the institution might not be subject to changes of political fortune, was the proviso that management, operation, and control would be vested in the museum's board of trustees rather than in the South Park commissioners. Quite sternly the contract concluded, "Museum regards last two conditions—the use of funds and the operation of the Museum—as indispensable conditions. Museum does not feel justified in receiving Mr. Rosenwald's contribution unless these conditions are definitely recognized." These important matters settled, Wormser predicted optimistically that reconstruction would start later in the year. He made his announcement as what he called "a fitting present" for Rosenwald's sixty-fifth birthday that August 12. Rosenwald was pleased but not sanguine, saying, "It is safer to be a historian than a prophet."

Wormser's hopes about when reconstruction would begin could not be realized because of delays in setting up specifications for bids to contractors and disagreements about structural details between some of the commissioners and Graham, the architect. But Wormser remained undaunted. In a long lecture to the Commercial Club, replete with slides about the Deutsches Museum and its innumerable attractions, he enunciated anew his philosophy that the new Museum's purpose was not only to exalt industry and technology and display their products but to aid the general public in understanding the social problems wrought by the swift pace of industrial progress over many decades and in comprehending the complex high-technology production and consumption. He drew considerable applause with his concluding remarks: "It is the function of an industrial museum to direct thought and not to leave meaningless man's conquest of the land, the waters and the air, of the means of communication, of material resources and power, but rather, with a full recognition of our debt to the past, to point these past achievements toward future potentialities. We shall dedicate our industrial museum in Chicago in this spirit, so that the din of the factory and the roar of the mills may not sound discords of materialism, but echo the harmony of applied science and progressive industrialism."

4.

There remained now, among other essential activity, the task of selecting an executive director. Throughout 1927 some three dozen candidates were considered for the vital position. In the midst of the search, Waldemar B. Kaempffert, science writer and editorialist for the New York *Times*, proposed inserting an advertisement in leading newspapers and science journals headed: "THE ROSENWALD INDUSTRIAL MUSEUM OF CHICAGO SEEKS AN EXECUTIVE DIRECTOR." The qualities required were many, according to Kaempffert's suggested ad copy: "He must have organizing and administrative ability of a high order. He must be well grounded in science and engineering and keenly aware of the part they have played in making the United States the greatest of industrial nations by freeing Americans from needless sweating and drudgery. He must have imagination—and courage to give that imagination full play. Something of the teacher there must be in him, something of the editor of a magazine addressed to the millions, something of the play-producer too. For the Rosenwald Industrial Museum is to be not a mausoleum of dead exhibits, but a place where the epic drama of industry's rise through science and technology is to be staged with the vividness of a living reality."

It soon developed that there was no need to place the proposed advertisement anywhere and that the logical man for the job was the man who had written the copy. Wormser was especially eager to have Kaempffert as director, for both men, along with Rosenwald, espoused the basic philosophy about the social meanings and implications—and complications—that technological and industrial developments bore within themselves. In March 1928 Wormser informed the board that Kaempffert would accept the twenty-thousand-dollar job, and on April 13, official announcement was made at a Commercial Club dinner in the Blackstone Hotel. Tall and imposing at fifty, with wavy hair and deep-set eyes, a connoisseur of good food and good wines, a much-traveled and learned man—in addition to writing books on astronomy, aeronautics, and American inventions, and scores of magazine articles, he was also a patent attorney—Kaempffert bristled with enthusiasm and vigor as he arose to acknowledge the appointment and orate about the future.

Inevitably he paid tribute to Dr. von Miller and the Deutsches Museum, which he had visited many times. The lights were darkened and the slides Wormser had shown at an earlier meeting were flashed on a screen while Kaempffert made witty and knowledgeable comments on exhibits ranging from the first Daimler automobile, of 1885, and an 1828 European railway coach to locomotives, balloons, dirigibles, and steam turbines. In his museum, he promised, everything would be on a grander scale. "We want to drive home the whole truth of modern mechanism. We want to show why it is that nowadays we press a button and any one of us will have—what? More candle power in our homes than Washington had at his inaugural ball, which was considered the most wonderfully illuminated of its kind that the world had ever seen." Paying shrewd tribute to the Commercial Club for its role in the museum project, he rumbled, "Gentlemen, it seems to me that we cannot help building here the greatest institution of its kind that this world is likely to see."

To reporters who clustered around him after the banquet, he continued to expound. "We will have the whirlwind motor which made it possible for Lindbergh to fly over the Atlantic. It will run. You will be able to stop and start it. We will show broadcasting, how a piece of soap is made. You will get into a covered wagon, then a stage coach, a day coach, a modern Pullman car. The main hall will be big enough for a locomotive to run up and down." Everywhere, there would be vivid life and motion to prevent typical "museum fatigue." The place would teem with action. "We will show how the industrial drama has evolved. The secret of movement. There will be no collection of mechanized fossils. You will feel yourself part of a great evolving industrial organism. We are going to have activity! Buttons to push! Levers and handles to turn! And nowhere any sign reading 'Hands Off'!"

Having spoken, Kaempffert announced plans for a six-month inspection of museums in London, Paris, Munich, and Vienna, promising that the first unit of his group to lay out the exhibits would shortly be set up. In traditional style, he divided the museum into basic sections, with a curator for each—physics and chemistry; geology, mining, and metallurgy; agriculture and forestry; motive power, civil engineering, and public works; and printing and graphic arts. He recruited for his staff such experts as Professor Andrew M. MacMahon of the University of Chicago's Ryerson Laboratory; John Robert Van Pelt, a geologist and mining engineer who would in time fill several crucial assignments at the Museum; Fred A. Lippold, a German marine engineer who had been briefly affiliated with the Deutsches Museum; Russell H. Anderson, an agricultural historian, and

A. C. Carlton and Herman Eberle, experienced mining engineers. A kinetic New York *Times* reporter, John A. Maloney, was lured from New York to handle public relations, and he quickly busied himself arranging interviews with Kaempffert that glowed with optimism and assurance. Maloney also joined in the chorus of predictions. "To me, the most interesting fact about this museum," he told the *Tribune*'s foremost feature writer, James O'Donnell Bennett, "is that it is going to be a double-header. It will have the finest exterior in the United States and an instructive and fascinating interior."

Upon his return from Europe early in 1929, Kaempffert continued to be characteristically effusive. To members of the Standard Club, he disclosed that various companies had promised nearly half a million dollars' worth of gifts, including an 1836 Illinois Central Railroad locomotive, the first horse-drawn streetcar ever used in Chicago, and a cutaway model of a modern Chicago Surface Lines streetcar; in its New York laboratories the Bell Telephone System was creating a full display to illustrate the development of telephonic communication. "That is what we thought would happen. Now we expect that in about ten years we shall have thirty million dollars' worth of exhibits reaching a distance of twelve miles, and about eighty per cent of them will be donated. . . . And it is our hope that in two or three years, when the corner stone of this building is ready to be laid, President Hoover, a great engineer under whom we believe we will have a greater advancement than we have ever had, will ride down Michigan boulevard with ten thousand men to officiate at that ceremony!"

CHAPTER III

MAJOR TRIBULATIONS, SLIGHT TRIUMPHS

Amid the euphoria there were vexing problems.

Initial bids for the rehabilitation of the exterior were scheduled to be asked for at the start of 1928, with Kelly giving assurances that work would definitely proceed a month later and Graham promising faithful reproduction of the original. But the commissioners dawdled and delayed, and neither they nor the trustees appeared to be disturbed by an announcement from New York, the city's perennial rival, that, after many years of procrastination, plans were finally afoot for a twenty million dollar Museum of the Peaceful Arts, with a financial starter in a three million dollar bequest in the 1924 will of Henry R. Towne, president of the Yale and Towne Lock Co. Not until May 16 were bids from five competing firms opened—and rejected, because all exceeded five million. On October 18, new bids still were too high and again were turned down; so were bids on December 19, although one was $350,000 below the five million dollar mark.

Further delay was occasioned in April by new litigation brought by William E. Furlong, seeking to restrain the South Park Board from carrying out the project. Although the Supreme Court had already ruled against him, Furlong repeated his original charge that the board had no legal authority to spend the money for building construction instead of for improvement of the parks themselves. He additionally alleged that the bond issue specified the money would be used for a convention hall and not for an industrial museum and that even if the bond issue were valid the commissioners had no power to authorize its management by what he described as "a private corporation." To the latter charge, Wormser offered the cogent counterargument that while the Rosenwald Industrial Museum indeed was a private corporation it had been incorporated not for pecuniary profit. As for the purposes for which the bond issue had been approved, Wormser carefully noted that these had included mention of an industrial museum "and such other uses advantageous to public interests as shall be practicable."

Judge Oscar Hebel turned down Furlong's request for an injunction, and within hours, $3,500,000 of the bonds issued were purchased by a major investment firm. Judge Hebel's decision, based mainly on the earlier Supreme Court ruling, also cleared the way for a new submission of bids. This time, on June 19—nearly three years after the first announcement of Rosenwald's largess—the assignment was finally awarded to the low bidder among nine firms, the R. C. Wieboldt Company, which had scaled its original bid down to $2,649,000.

And still there were delays. When Kelly announced in July that terra cotta instead of limestone would be used on the exterior of the building to save an estimated three hundred thousand dollars in construction costs, some architects, artists, and civic groups inveighed against the plan. Lorado Taft shuddered at the proposal, and Commissioner Igoe agreed: "No woman could be persuaded to accept an imitation pearl if she could afford the genuine." The *Tribune* was horrified: "Terra cotta is an excellent material for many purposes, and in many cases it is exclusively proper material,

but for Chicago's only public building of unique architectural importance it would be tragically inappropriate."

Construction companies specializing in terra cotta joined
in the debate. Several took full-page advertisements in the
newspapers, of which that of the Midland Terra Cotta Company was typical. It emphasized the fondness of the an-
cients for terra cotta—"The granaries, storehouses and records of Egypt, the aqueducts and other remains of Roman
times testify how widespread was its use"—and added, "The
artists of the Renaissance left such beautiful examples of
terra cotta as the Cathedral of Monza, the Certosa near
Pavia, and no sculptural work of the great fifteenth century
ever surpassed the Singing Gallery done by Luca della Rob-
bia for the Cathedral of Florence in 1430. . . . In England,
the friezes, cornices and other high ornamental work of
the Tudor period were of terra cotta." It even called on the
shade of Daniel H. Burnham to testify as "one of the first
and most consistent users of architectural terra cotta."

The conflicts, major and minor, annoyed Rosenwald. To
resolve the matter of costs, he authorized Wormser to make
public his offer to fulfill any deficit incurred in the rehabilitation up to one million dollars, in addition to the amount
specified in his original agreement with the South Park
Board. And he brought to a conclusion his persistent campaign to remove his name.

Only in two previous instances had he permitted his name
to be so used. One was Julius Rosenwald Hall, constructed
on the University of Chicago campus in 1914 to house the
departments of geology and geography, and the other was
the Rosenwald Library established in Luxor, Egypt, in 1926,
as part of the research facilities of the university's Oriental
Institute. In each case, his name was applied to only one
building among many, for Rosenwald felt that this limited
use would not inhibit other benefactions. But he believed—
and often stated emphatically—that to name an entire in-

stitution for one philanthropist might well lead the public to expect the donor to meet all the institution's needs and discourage other potential gift givers.

Rosenwald kept peppering Wormser and the trustees with his requests until they acceded on July 3 by formally changing the name to Museum of Science and Industry, but adding that it always be followed by "Founded by Julius Rosenwald." Reaction to the alteration was universally favorable, best exemplified by an editorial in the New York *Times*, which commended Rosenwald for becoming modesty by this act of self-effacement. Emphasizing that ultimately the Museum would represent an investment ten times the sum Rosenwald had set up for it, the editorial commented, "Mr. Rosenwald regards himself primarily as an instrument in carrying out an idea in visual education new to this country. Thus he sets a new example in philanthropy."

As for the terra cotta limestone imbrogolio, it was settled early in September by a decision to use Indiana limestone for the exterior and granite for the outside stairs, with the dome of the central hall finished in terra cotta. After the contract with the R. C. Wieboldt Company was formally signed, Kelly announced that work would begin at once and be completed in eighteen months, and again he and other commissioners and park district officials trekked out to the noble ruin, there to pose wielding a pick on the stucco molding around one of the massive columns. Sighing editorially with relief at the promise of progress, the *Tribune* once again praised the enterprise and its prime supporter: "The successful outcome of the struggle to reclaim the building is an important event in the life of the city and the nation. . . . While the institution does not bear Mr. Rosenwald's name, it will be universally known as the Rosenwald Museum. There is no philanthropist in our generation who so richly merits the honor of having his name linked with one of the nation's great educational institutions."

At year's end Dr. Oskar von Miller came to the city to observe the progress being made in renovation and to give his blessing. He learned from Kaempffert that in that troubled year an additional half million dollars' worth of exhibits had been pledged, among the accessions a length of pipe laid in London in 1630, a bus that had traveled 750,000 miles through many years between New Orleans and Chicago, the apparatus Professor Albert A. Michelson had used to measure the velocity of light, the carriage in which President and Mrs. McKinley had ridden to and from the White House in 1899, and the four original models of the "soaring machines" of the pioneer airplane builder Dr. Octave Chanute.

2.

One final legal barrier remained. Undaunted, Furlong had appealed Judge Hebel's decision to the State Supreme Court. He sought to strengthen his basic arguments by maintaining that Illinois's constitution prohibited municipalities from making donations to private corporations and that the South Park Board's granting of permission to the Museum to use a building constructed in part by public funds constituted such a donation. In a forceful reply Wormser argued that the constitutional prohibition was aimed at donations by municipalities to railroads and that Furlong's action was "an attack upon a great public project made possible by a munificent private gift." He disclosed, too, that Rosenwald was ready to increase his additional funds for rehabilitation to between one and a half and two million dollars if necessary, thereby making his total contribution close to five million dollars. Again the high court turned back Furlong in a ruling on June 21, 1930. "It strikes us very forcibly," its decision read, "that the park commissioners were acting in the public interest. . . . The benefits to the public of such a Museum are not denied, and the public have the proposal of Julius Rosenwald, a public-spirited, philanthropic man, to contribute approximately $3,000,000 for the public good in conducting the Museum. We do not think the commissioners have violated any rule of law or the constitution in passing the ordinance and entering the contract."

Kaempffert was delighted. "There is no further step Mr. Furlong can take," he said. "We have been proceeding slowly and cautiously, but now we can push forward with the utmost rapidity." The architectural firm of Shaw, Naess, and Murphy had been signed to work with Ernest Graham's company in designing the interior. Kaempffert assigned Van Pelt, who earlier that year had gone to Europe to gain ideas and establish contacts at the Deutsches Museum and others in Europe, as liaison with the architects to assure development of the kind of industrial museum he envisioned instead of a traditionally static, display-type institution.

Plans devised by the architectural firm's Alfred P. Shaw called for constructing two balconies in place of the one existing since the days of the World's Columbian Exposition and building a floor strong enough to sustain heavy engines and other exhibits. The new first-floor level would be established almost five feet higher than its old level and would be reached by additional broad steps inside the entrance. Beneath it and throughout the entire building the ground was to be excavated, thereby gaining six additional acres of floor space. A number of interior supporting walls were to be replaced with steel columns, and the glass skylights that covered the greater part of the roof of the old buildings, except for those atop the business office, library, and certain studios, with solid roofing material of tile and copper. When finished, the reconstructed building would, like its original, contain thirteen million cubic feet. Two thirds of the six hundred thousand square feet of total floor space would be available for exhibits and the rest for offices, library, cafeteria, private dining room, kitchens, shops, and a receiving room, the latter below ground level. In the west pavilion, beyond allotted space for exhibits, would be an auditorium with one thousand seats and beneath it a three hundred-seat lecture hall. Work on the exterior continued through 1930, and by October, 90 per cent of it, with limestone facing, ornamentation, and columns, had been completed and hopes were high that remodeling of the interior would soon proceed.

John Maloney made certain that every activity was well reported. Both he and Kaempffert were eager for as much publicity as possible, keeping in mind Dr. von Miller's dictum, "The Museum must be made known even in the most far-reaching districts," and aware that articles in newspapers and trade journals served to supplement speeches and personal visits to corporations and individuals from whom money or exhibits might be forthcoming. During 1930 no fewer than six hundred newspaper stories, averaging a column long, appeared, in addition to thirty articles in general magazines and trade journals and in specialized publications ranging from London's *The British Printer*, which acclaimed the formation of a department of graphic arts, with examples of early forms of recorded communication, tablets, manuscripts, and block printing, to the *Northwestern Alumni News*, which proudly noted that J. B. Hayford, Engineering '23, was the institution's business manager. Photographs and sketches of work in progress appeared persistently in magazine sections and on picture pages of the city's newspapers with captions invariably reading "Art Prepares a Shrine for Industry" or "The Restoration of a Masterpiece" or "A Rare Jewel."

Crowds were attracted to the site, and weekend painters and amateur photographers assiduously recorded the prog-

ress being made; occasionally children waded in the
fringes of the south lagoon, and on at least one occasion an
elderly man was spied fishing there for tiny bluegills. Frank
L. Hayes, a *Daily News* writer assigned to report regularly
on the project, took note of the inevitable crowds watching
workmen and construction crews and was moved to verse:

> "Why are the people stopping here?" the
> Crowds-at-Lunch-Hour sigh.
> "To kill some time," the Cynic makes reply.
> But his reproach is answered by a scientist's apology:
> "The group is actuated by a hunger for technology
> When watching excavations during noon-time."

Duly recorded were acquisitions that came or were promised the Museum. The Pullman Car Works, from the model
city on Chicago's far South Side, sent along a duplicate of
the vestibule first used on all Pullman cars forty-three years
earlier. From Freeman Gosden and Charles Correll—the
popular Amos 'n' Andy radio team—came an 1883-model
double-keyboard typewriter they had received from one of
their listeners. Kaempffert made a plea for historically important items, although, as he informed reporters who called
regularly on him, "We have plenty of old-fashioned hand
looms and I won't take another spinning wheel as a gift."
What he especially wanted, he said, was a hand printing
press, an original Howe sewing machine, or an early automobile of the kind that was ordered off the streets of
Chicago because it was too dangerous. A Philadelphia antiques expert, M. L. Blumenthal, was employed to scour
farmhouses, barns, and dwellings in villages in New England states and appeared regularly at every county fair and
auction he could get to, so that, despite Kaempffert's desire
to have no more hand looms or old teapots, such objects and
similar relics kept arriving and were duly stored in nearby
warehouses.

3.

As the new year began, Kaempffert unexpectedly offered his resignation as executive director, expressing a desire to return to the New York *Times* as science editor. There were reports among staff members that he had chafed under directives compelling him to make detailed periodic reports to the trustees and to receive the approval of a newly formed executive committee before making expenditures for acquisitions, but his departure was without rancor and he promised to fulfill an agreement to write the text for a booklet, *From Cave-man to Engineer*, that was being planned for publication on the Museum's official opening.

Van Pelt, who had worked so closely with Kaempffert in devising the sequential layout of exhibits and in supervising carefully the architectural and engineering complexities of the over-all project, was appointed acting director. Although he had little experience as an administrator, Van Pelt carried out his duties ably, conferring far more frequently with President Avery than the independent-minded Kaempffert had been accustomed to do and continuing with staff members to define and advance exhibit plans. The first effects of the stock-market crash of October 1929 were beginning to be felt, but Wormser advised Van Pelt not to worry about funds and concentrate on exhibits and construction.

Meanwhile the quest proceeded for Kaempffert's successor. Five months later, after considering some forty candidates, the trustees picked Otto Theo Kreusser, director of engineering tests for the General Motors Corporation, a hearty, exuberant man who was highly regarded in engineering circles and was a protégé of Charles F. Kettering, General Motors' famous "Boss Ket." William Rufus Abbott, who had recently succeeded Sewell Avery as the Museum's president, described Kreusser as "a brainy man with a wallop," and the new director promptly expressed confidence as he assumed his duties that under his aegis the Museum would have special appeal to the nation's young: "The accumulated knowledge in the place would have taken the parents of the children who will see it 20 years of tedious research and study to acquire. But we plan to put all that at the finger tips of the next generation, with the added asset of actually seeing all these machines working. In this way we hope the Museum will bring out three or four great inventive minds during a generation."

As in the preceding months, the task of securing materials for exhibits continued, and periodic reports issued from Kreusser and Maloney about interesting and instructive acquisitions. Under Kaempffert, no great strides had been taken in directly soliciting industries all over the country. Even when such solicitations had been made, the response had been rather meager because of the economic straits in which many companies increasingly found themselves since the start of the Great Depression. Not only was he going to seek industry's aid, Kreusser told an *Evening Post* reporter—who, unfortunately, referred to him as "Krueger" throughout his story—but he hoped that one of the lessons that might be shown at the Museum would be the dangers of overproduction, a contributing factor to the economic slump. "We would also help young men find their place in the world by allowing them the opportunity to study the work in which they would like to engage instead of having them drift from job to job in an effort to find employment to their liking."

Whatever success or lack of it Kreusser had in persuading large and small firms to make contributions was made evident in the variety of items whose acquisition was announced in ensuing months. Fred W. Sargent, president of the Chicago and North Western Railway, turned over a collection of 143 historical relics that included strap rails and pins used to hook old-style cars together, detailed plans of the first bridge built across the Mississippi River in 1864, dozens of old timetables, record books, and photographs. Members of the glassmaking industry promised support for an exhibit narrating the manufacture of glass through the centuries right down to a glass-melting furnace. Libby, McNeill & Libby sent a dozen fifty-year-old cans of soup that had been carried by a relief expedition in 1883 to Major General A. W. Greeley when that famed explorer's party had been bogged down in the Arctic. Through the efforts of Dr. Max Henius, United Danish Distillers of Copenhagen contributed a model distillery that had taken two years to build at a cost of twenty thousand dollars, and a model of a brewery originally built for the International Brewers' Congress in 1911 was reconditioned for exhibit at the Museum. Transferred to Chicago from Panama was a ten-foot section of the old Las Cruces Trail, over which had been carried treasure wrested from the natives of Central and South America during Spanish colonial times and gold from California in 1849. Added to these variegated items were such curios as an ancient meat pounder, an 1840 hoop tightener, an 1830 compass plane, an 1883 wall telephone, an 1850 leather valise, an 1850 miners' lamp, a holystone used to scrub ship decks, a wrought-iron anchor, 1868 mining stock certificates, old paper money, and defunct railroad bonds.

Most anticipated of all exhibits was a working coal mine. This project was principally Kreusser's idea. Early in his term he had vigorously proposed that the Museum aim for a 1933 opening—if only of a sample section—to coincide with the massive lakefront exposition called A Century of Progress, so that the hordes of expected visitors there could be made aware of the Museum and be stimulated to visit it. To attract them, he further proposed, a spectacular attraction was necessary, whether or not it fitted in with Kaempffert's basic sequential-exhibit philosophy.

Because of Van Pelt's experience as a mining engineer,

Kreusser asked him to drop all other duties except the periodic conferences with the architects and supervise the design and construction of a mine typical of those in southern Illinois that could take visitors down its shaft sixty-five feet below to watch authentic miners performing various kinds of mining operations.

Initially there were difficulties. Kreusser's enthusiasm over this project ran so persistently high that he did not keep the trustees fully informed of all the details—including the ultimate cost to the Museum of at least $250,000, an amount that would have to be equaled by contributions from industries involved in all aspects of mining operations. Consequently, when he came before the board for such funds to pay for the construction of what had been so patiently and carefully designed, he was confronted with considerable opposition. Kreusser suggested formation of a committee of imaginative and top-ranking men in the fields of mining, geology, and metallurgy to examine and evaluate not only the plans for the coal mine but the entire sequence of exhibits in their particular fields. The result was overwhelming approval by these experts, many of whom were instrumental in persuading companies in which they held vital positions to help finance the project and supply needed machinery and equipment.

Van Pelt not only was in over-all charge, but in at least one important instance made a crucial contribution. After several elevator companies shied away from attempting to design the hoisting machinery and shaft headframe as too risky, he devised a workable system that ultimately was used by the Otis Elevator Company in carrying out the essential task.

In addition, during the first year of Kreusser's term, two relationships of importance to the future of the Museum were established. The first was an agreement with officials of A Century of Progress by which various Museum curators and scientists would aid in preparing scientific and industrial exhibits; in exchange, exhibits there would be given to the Museum after the end of the fair along with 25 per cent of all surplus funds that remained. The second was an arrangement with the University of Chicago by which students taking the general survey course in the physical sciences would be permitted and encouraged to come to the Museum to observe in action and motion some of the principles in the course syllabus; at the university's laboratory school, Professor MacMahon, the Museum's physics curator, was building an exhibit that would, through the use of magnets, electric batteries, railway trains on toy tracks, and other devices, graphically illustrate the laws of motion, the movements of planets and stars, and the speed of light. In subsequent years, these relationships would expand considerably and play crucial parts in the Museum's history and growth.

4.

As the Museum moved toward its opening date, in the midst of worries about the deepening economic depression, Rosenwald's generosity prevailed and expanded. In line with his promise to supply additional money when necessary, in May 1931 he augmented the original three million dollars he had donated in 1929 with ten thousand shares of Sears Roebuck and Co. stock at seventy-five dollars a share, and in October twenty thousand additional shares at forty-two dollars each. The total holdings, he estimated, would yield at least $150,000 in annual dividends. When Abbott expressed apprehension over a lack of sources of money for anticipated expenditures of some six hundred thousand dollars a year, Rosenwald suggested a program of memberships, and Wormser proposed drafting a bill that would enable the Museum to benefit from a state museum tax. The membership idea proved impractical at that time. The museum tax bill was drafted, but it did not pass until several years after

Edward J. Kelly became Chicago's mayor in 1933 and could exert considerable influence on members of his Democratic organization in the state legislature. (When the bill, drafted by Willard L. King, a scholarly lawyer in Wormser's office, failed to pass on its first effort, Colonel Alfred A. Sprague, one of the earliest Commercial Club backers of the Museum, asked the mayor for help. The reply was, "Why should I front for that Museum?" Sprague pointed to Kelly's signature on the original contract between the South Park Board and the Museum and read him the clause to the effect that both would co-operate in getting such legislation approved. Kelly then agreed to use his not inconsiderable powers as a party chieftain to gain passage of the amended bill.)

Rosenwald envisaged additional revenues from individuals, corporations, and educational foundations, but in a "Dear Rufus" letter to Abbott he wrote that he was realistic enough to know that such a time was some distance away and that stock dividends and Museum tax receipts would not be sufficient in the meantime for the upkeep of the Museum: "I realize that I may well be expected to bear a substantial part of the maintenance deficit and that is my intention, provided the trustees are as conscientious in their expenditures as the present ones are." In view of his past actions and voluntary obligations to the Museum, he concluded, he did not think it necessary to make any more definite commitments. "But I will see to it that the Museum is well provided for."

Even as he sent his letter, Rosenwald was seriously ill with arteriosclerosis complicated by heart disease and a kidney ailment. Although he grew progressively worse, he made alterations in his will that would bear out his assurance to Abbott, and these were made known in the days after he died at sixty-nine, on the afternoon of January 6, 1932, in his home in the Chicago suburb of Ravinia. Editorials by the hundreds all over the country lauded his humanitarianism and business acumen and enumerated his innumerable gifts to charity, public health, housing, and education, which surpassed sixty-two million dollars.

When, a week later, the details of his will were made public, it was disclosed that less than a month before his death, he had directed that another eleven million dollars of his fortune be diverted to philanthropic purposes through the newly formed Rosenwald Family Association, of which his five children were named trustees, with the proviso that adequate sums be made available for the benefit of the Museum. Eventually an additional $3,491,000 came from this source by 1935, and this, with a final gift of $125,000 in 1944, brought the total contributions from the great philanthropist to close to seven million dollars. In stark contrast, cash gifts in that span of years to the Museum from all other individuals amounted to only fifteen thousand dollars.

But in the immediate wake of Rosenwald's death, in 1932, while allotted funds were still tied up in Probate Court, the Museum was in a stringent financial condition. Work on the interior was halted with less than one tenth completed, and other economies went into effect, including a cut in personnel from eighty-eight to twenty-two, with a 10 per cent salary cut for those remaining, a reduction in office space for Kreusser, Hayford, the young business manager, and the curators and remaining staff members on the ninth floor of the Hyde Park-Kenwood National Bank Building, and a voluntary 40 per cent slash in Kreusser's salary and one of 25 per cent for Van Pelt. At a special staff meeting, Kreusser spoke movingly and frankly about the Museum's financial plight, offered aid to discharged employees in finding other jobs, and explained the need for the salary cuts—without citing the far greater amount by which he had cut his own. And, with drastic economies in effect and trustees' directives to keep all spending at absolute minimums, the Museum limped ahead to its scheduled opening.

CHAPTER IV

A COAL MINE AND OTHER WONDERS

Despite the precarious financial state and the largely un-
completed condition of the interior, Kreusser was determined to open the Museum in the early summer of 1933 not
only because advance publicity had buoyantly promised it
but to fulfill his goal of enticing visitors in the city for A
Century of Progress. Invitations that went out for a special
preview on June 19, less than three weeks after the colorful
lakefront fair opened its gates, specified that visitors would
see only "the first unit" of the Museum, essentially a portion
of the central hall and the south and north courts. In other
sections loomed steel girders and all the paraphernalia of
construction, and the floor on which exhibits were placed
was simply a slab of poured concrete with steel reinforcing
rods sticking through. Amid these makeshift surroundings
and facing a large oil portrait of the Museum's prime bene-
factor, painted by John Doctoroff from photographs because
Rosenwald had shied away from posing formally, two hundred guests gathered—among them another Rosenwald son,
Lessing, and the philanthropist's widow and her three grandchildren, Thomas Goodkind, Allen Felsenthal, and little
Adele Stern, who referred to the Museum as "granddaddy's
house"—to hear brief comments by Abbott ("What the Museum presents now is a cross-section of what it will ulti-

mately become") and Mayor Kelly ("There were many trials and tribulations, but praise be that we have it today!").

What they and thousands who came on the July 1 official opening day saw was considerably less than all the pre-opening publicity had promised. In the north court, embellished with eleven murals by David Leavitt artistically summarizing a score of man's achievements in many areas from architecture to transportation, the prime attraction appeared to be a papier-mâché cow. To it was attached a modern suction-pump milking machine, and with the turn of a key it swished its tail, chewed its cud, and turned its head as milk poured into a glass receptacle. In a small agricultural exhibit was a modern horse-drawn checkrow corn planter and a miniature of a steam traction engine and machine used for threshing wheat, oats, rice, and peas.

Past the entrance to the central hall, where a mural by Nicholas Remisoff symbolized agriculture, architecture, transportation, and communication, stood the Arkwright spinning frame depicting the first harnessing of a steam engine for spinning by machinery, and across the way an 1820 Washington hand printing press. A deep-sea diving suit on a manikin drew visitors toward a large water-filled glass tank in which a real diver demonstrated with an acetylene torch on a sheet of metal the method used to cut through sunken ships to salvage cargo. In a rudimentary transportation display was a replica of the famed Rocket, the "grandfather of all locomotives," built in the 1820s by George and Robert Stephenson; the Rocket had won the famous Rainhill trials in 1829 near Liverpool, England, to test whether horses, fixed engines with cables, or locomotives were best for use on the new Liverpool and Manchester Railroad. Nearby were highway crossing signals and an airplane pilot trainer. There were push-button devices to illustrate how sound travels, how music is made, lightning is produced and momentum is sustained, and a variety of machines animatedly illustrating other principles of the physical sciences.

Beyond doubt, the major attraction was the coal mine. There had been one final problem on the day before the preview: the passenger train in the mine, pulled by a chain-link system operating through a slot between the rails, had just been completed, and on the first trials it jumped the track with irritating regularity. Kreusser, immediately aware that the train was not heavy enough to stay on the track without passengers, ordered sandbags placed beneath enough seats so that when the trustees took their first ride, the train moved without mishap.

The public response to the coal mine was instantly favorable, although it is doubtful any description could match, for rhapsodic rhetoric, Kaempffert's in *From Cave-man to Engineer:* "It is impossible to distinguish reality from illusion here. The mine-cage and coal-skip appear alternately at three-minute intervals at the top of the head-frame, the skip dumping seven tons of coal which it has raised. Climb the stairs around the head-frame and step into the cage. It is the miner's elevator, far older than the elevator that takes you to and from your skyscraper office. The cage seems to drop a distance of 500 feet, the length of the cable. There is a blast of cold air and a musty smell, both inseparable from coal-mining. Ears, eyes, nose, skin—every sense proclaims the coal mine. At the bottom of the shaft you step out. Here is a pump room. Water trickles in through ditches. See the pump suck it up and then realize what it has always meant to keep a mine dry. In this office—it is the superintendent's—are charts. Glance at them. They indicate, as in actual practice, the general plan of the mine and the location of miners and machines. . . . Farther on is a rotary dump. Watch it turn a full-sized car upside down and right it empty. Up this short ramp now to a mine train—an electric locomotive and two cars. Take a seat in one of the cars. You are off for a trip through the mine.

"Three minutes in semi-darkness and the train stops. You are now at a working face of coal. The motorman (call him

that if you like) leaves the locomotive, to demonstrate a
short-wall cutter and a coal-getter in a low seam. You understand now why coal is plentiful and cheap—why much of
the old drudgery of winning it with the pick and drill be-
longs to the inefficient past. . . . The train moves on. You
come to a room that has already been mined, a room-and-
pillar mine, so-called because of the pillars of coal left standing to hold up the roof above. Here is another type of coal-
cutting machine. A Jeffery arc-wall cutter, it is called. It
makes cuts ten feet wide. A Joy loader stretches out its arms
to gather coal and convey it to a car drawn by a gathering
locomotive. There's a post-drill, too, preparing the holes into
which explosive will be tapped after the day-shift goes.

"You leave the room-and-pillar mine and walk up the
counter-gangway of an inclined-seam mine typical of the
state of Washington. Look down and you see chutes pitched
at an angle of 40 degrees, chutes that have been worked. You
learn thus still another method of wresting coal from the
ground—this time from strata that nature has tilted at an
awkward angle. Out now by way of a temporary exit stairway and you find yourself on the main floor of the Museum
again."

In some of the exhibits, recorded lectures described their
workings, but most of the explanations and demonstrations
were conducted by a corps of thirty-five demonstrators—
later called "guide-lecturers"—recruited mostly from nearby
universities, where they were studying for higher degrees.
One of them was a young University of Chicago student,
Daniel M. MacMaster, assigned to the graphic arts department to talk about the printing presses but destined to play a
far more important part in the Museum's history in ensuing
years. MacMaster and his colleagues received only fifty
cents an hour, slightly lower than the amount received by
the "coal miners," some of whom were mining engineers willing to work at low wages because jobs in their field were not
available in this period of the economic depression.

Under the tutelage of A. C. Carlton, who was also curator of mining, they worked with zeal and efficiency, but their
efforts were not enough to still criticism from some visitors
that the Museum had failed to live up to preliminary bally-
hoo. A Chicagoan, C. Z. Dillenbeck, altered the name of the
institution in an irate letter to the *Tribune* and complained,
"A visit to the Museum of Science and Invention leads one
to wonder what has happened here. The only real exhibit is
that of coal handling machinery and a few electrical devices,
most of which are applicable to any factor. The interior of
the building is entirely unfinished and if memory serves me
right a bond issue of two million or more dollars was made
expressly for the interior work. General indications are that
we are a very long way from having a Museum of Science
and Invention." Maloney made a swift reply, correcting Dillenbeck's several errors and chiding him for evidently not
spending enough time at the Museum to see the coal mine
and two hundred other exhibits "which represent many
thousands of dollars spent by Chicago and industries which
know that it will be in a few years' time the largest and best
technical Museum in the world." There had never been any
intention to open the entire Museum at one time, he claimed,
and added, "Twelve miles of exhibits covering every phase
of man's scientific and engineering activity cannot be properly installed overnight." As for the indignant citizen's
doubts that the Museum had fulfilled any of its original purposes, Maloney urged, "If he doubts the Museum's growing
popularity, let him try to find parking space in front of it
next Sunday."

2.

As if to attest to Maloney's assertion about the Museum's
popularity, total attendance by the end of August was over
a hundred thousand. Many were out-of-town visitors to A

Century of Progress, thereby attesting to the astuteness of those who had insisted on a summer opening. In succeeding weeks the attendance maintained its pace; among the distinguished guests was Guglielmo Marconi, the famed inventor, who spent a quick hour of a busy stay in the city and posed with his wife and Wormser listening at the sound-focusing exhibit to an alarm clock ticking at a distance of thirty feet.

When the fair shut down for the year in October, Museum attendance slackened. The need for economy still prevailed, although the Rosenwald heirs approved an additional six hundred thousand dollars from the estate. Several trustees gave consideration to closing the Museum in the late fall and winter months because the building as yet lacked a central heating system. Kreusser successfully opposed the idea, asserting that temporary heating could be installed and partitions erected to separate the central passageway with its exhibits from the rest of the building, where construction was continuing. He thereupon arranged to place around the edges of the exhibit areas steel drums containing coke, similar to salamanders used in buildings under construction to keep concrete and plaster from freezing. They were quite crude in appearance, but as a temporary measure were serviceable enough. On one of his visits, Kreusser stood so close to one of the coke containers that when he got his trousers back from the cleaners they were split down the middle at the crease, for he had literally baked them. His tart suggestion that small white fences be placed around the steel drums was quickly acted upon.

Those who did venture out to the Museum found more to interest them: an "electric eye" in the form of a photoelectric cell that was used to sort cans of evaporated milk; a fifteen-foot torpedo with compressed-air tank, turbine, and gyroscope; an ancestor of television in a photoelectric device that transmitted pictures of Alfred E. Smith and Greta Garbo; the spherical gondola in which Marine Major Chester Fordney and Lieutenant Commander Thomas Settle had recently made their 62,000-foot record flight into the stratosphere, and a replica of Eli Whitney's cotton gin.

Increasingly the coal mine was the prime attraction ("Old King Coal Draws Many to Mine at Museum," read a *Daily News* headline). As the depression persisted, hardly a day passed that Alice Depogny, an accountant doubling as a cashier at the coal mine, was not asked by someone at the tour's conclusion where he might place an order for coal and what the charges were. In the south court stood an extensive collection of mining equipment and a series of charts portraying the industrial history of coal starting with its use by the ancient Greeks in 300 B.C. And long after most of the opening exhibits would be discarded, the coal mine would continue to be a major lure for visitors and yield revenues (at the start, twenty-five cents for adults and ten cents for children).

At year's end, the attendance totaled close to three hundred thousand, and all involved in the effort to put even a small part of it on public view were reasonably satisfied.

3.

The stratospheric gondola that had been placed on exhibit late in the year had come from A Century of Progress in accord with the earlier agreement, and now other exhibits began to trickle into the Museum from the lakefront fair. Chief among these was the "Epic of Meat," one of the most popular attractions at the fair's Agricultural Building and the joint effort of virtually all the packing, stockyards, and livestock industries in the country. Fronted by a diorama showing a cowboy on his pony surveying a vast cattle ranch, the exhibit included a completely equipped refrigerator and other cooling devices and a cutting table containing various wholesale meat cuts and carcasses of beef, pork, and lamb hung from overhead trolleys, plus an assortment of white, glassed cases showing, to the delight of women viewers, every kind of fancy cut and arrangement of meats for the dining table.

This exhibit sustained its popularity at the Museum, as did another new display of a hundred examples of industrial art, from gleaming pots and pans to furnaces and dental drills, secured from New York's Museum of Modern Art largely through the efforts of Alfred Shaw, the architect whose interior designs were slowly being carried out throughout the rest of the building. Kreusser was hopeful, he told reporters, that the display would help the public appreciate the "logical beauty of machine art, dependent upon lines and masses and colors and textures and not upon unnecessary ornamentation" and that with this appreciation would come a demand for increased beauty in all industrial products.

Earlier in 1933 a major change had occurred in the Museum's officialdom with the election of Rufus C. Dawes as the Museum's new president. He continued to devote his time and energies to the lakefront fair until it came to an end on October 1, when he assumed full duties at the Museum at twenty-five thousand dollars a year. Widely known as an able business executive, he had been highly active in earlier years in the promotion and management of public-utility companies, and with his brother, Charles, the famous Army general who later served as vice-president under President Coolidge, had organized the massive Central Trust Company of Chicago and helped administer the Dawes Plan for the payment of German reparations after the First World War. His tenure as president of A Century of Progress in its first season of operation had been gratifyingly successful, abetted considerably by the efficient and tightly organized efforts of the fair's general manager, a peppery Army major named Lenox R. Lohr. "If Julius Rosenwald were here today," said Wormser when asked for comment on the election, "Rufus Dawes is the man he would select as president of the

Museum. With a name internationally known and with a record respected throughout this country, Mr. Dawes will bring prestige to the Museum and will make it pre-eminent."

Dawes's affiliation with the Museum definitely assured the eventual transfer of scores of important exhibits from the fair by sponsors whose catalogue, as Malcolm McDowell, the *Daily News* reporter at the fair, wrote, "reads like a blue book of American science and industry." Dr. Eben J. Carey, the director of the vastly popular medical exhibits in the fair's Hall of Science, co-operated with Dawes in persuading his exhibitors to shift their displays to the Museum. Less than twelve hours after the fair officially ended, the first of the direct shipments to the Museum was made—a big American Petroleum Institute oil-well rig that had been seen by millions. This started a procession of huge trucks with the rest of the oil industry's exhibit. Room had been cleared by removing to warehouses most of the exhibits that had been seen at the Museum's opening, and in rapid succession during the rest of October there followed into the Museum the periodic table of the elements from the Hall of Science, the model of a phosphate plant displayed by the Victor Chemical Company, the Radio Corporation of America's facsimile of the wireless transmission of pictures, the oscilloscope from the American Telephone and Telegraph Company's exhibit in the Electrical Building, the Merck exhibit showing the growth of crystals, the General Electric steam turbine, the sugar-refinery model of the National Sugar Refining Company, the diorama of the Norfolk & Western Railroad from the Travel and Transport Building, and even six wooden figures carved by Carl Halsthammer of automobile artisans, which had been displayed in the General Motors Building.

At least two hundred other exhibits awaited the trucks—and space. But completion of the rest of the interior of the building had been delayed by the tragic death of Leo Wormser in an automobile accident in Michigan late that summer. Consequently a rotation system was established throughout 1934 until more space would become available for permanent positions. A woven-wire fence was stretched across the east end of the second floor of the fair's Hall of Science, behind which day-and-night guards watched over exhibits that included 110 physics displays, seventy-five chemical units, fifty biological and fifty geological exhibits, and parts of the medical, dental, and pharmacy sections, until their time for moving to the Museum was set according to the plan of rotation.

When special guests and visitors, contemplating the seemingly constant movement and shifting and replacement of exhibits while workmen continued to weld and plaster and paint elsewhere in the building, asked, "When will the Museum be finished?" Kreusser had an invariable reply: "Never! The Museum always will be in a state of growth." Philip Kinsley, the *Tribune*'s brilliant science writer, paid a visit early in June 1935, and although he noted that the interior was still only about one eighth completed, he reported Kreusser's prediction that eventually three million persons a year would come to the Museum. "It is evolving slowly into a great and unique sequence of Museums," Kinsley concluded, "in which the story of mankind from caveman to engineer may be learned in a way that words can never teach."

4.

To speed the completion of the Museum, the trustees early in 1936 voted to sell ten thousand shares of Sears Roebuck and Co. stock at not less than sixty dollars a share. This, plus amounts accruing from further sale of South Park bonds and revenues from the coal mine, was deemed sufficient to take care of costs of carrying on the necessary work. Kreusser made valiant efforts to interest various industrial firms beyond those which had authorized transfer of their Century of Progress exhibits, to subsidize new ventures. But he was largely unsuccessful, because most firms still had economic woes, and those not so burdened were not greatly interested in making substantial investments in an institution whose annual attendance continued to hover around three hundred thousand and showed few signs of rising. He often stayed in his temporary offices long after the six o'clock closing hour, drafting letters soliciting contributions from industrialists.

To stimulate attendance, attempts were made to interest Chicago schools in sending organized groups. But they proved largely fruitless. When MacMaster called on principals in nearly every major school in the city to make skillful presentations designed to persuade them to undertake student tours, he was invariably told that they faced more critical, immediate matters—for one, seeing that the children did not faint in class from lack of food and milk—and thoughts about securing resources for bus trips to the Museum were then impractical.

That autumn, Kreusser informed the trustees that he had been offered an important job in the research division of the General Motors Corporation and was eager to accept it. Again Van Pelt assumed temporary duties as director, and again a search was carried on for the man who would be the Museum's third director. This time the choice was closer to home. In April 1937 Dr. Philip Fox, for eight years director of the Adler Planetarium on the city's Northerly Island, was appointed Kreusser's successor at fifteen thousand dollars a year. An Army major in World War I and later a reserve colonel, he had gained considerable prominence, before becoming the planetarium's first chief, as professor of astronomy at Northwestern University and director of its Dearborn Observatory. During the Century of Progress fair he had worked closely with Dawes in making planetarium facilities available to visitors to the nearby exposition; he had helped to carry out the spectacular feat of having the fair lights turned on with impulses sent out forty years earlier by the star Arcturus, and his daily talk on "Drama of the Heavens," delivered under the planetarium's dome, had been heard by hundreds of thousands of fair visitors.

In crisp army style, Fox convened curators and other Museum personnel. "I'm a new man, but I don't intend to sweep with a new broom," he told them. "Of course, we work five days a week, but on the other hand it would be a good idea for anyone who wants to, and it would be looked on with favor, to work on Saturday too." He himself kept long hours and insisted on opening his own mail instead of having his secretary do so. To many, he seemed less concerned with attracting larger crowds than with converting the Museum into an institution for scholars and educators, and he gave the general impression of being more interested in his specialized field of binary stars than in most of the existing Museum exhibits. His main function, as he saw it, was to supervise the completion of the Museum and with his aides and curators to make detailed long-range plans for exhibits to be acquired. As work progressed on the interior, he took a greater interest in the basic purposes for which the Museum had been organized. In a new monthly publication, rather academically titled *Notes*, he wrote that it would contain not only a chronicle of activities but technical and scientific articles to give *Notes* more than ephemeral value and reflect the underlying purpose of the Museum itself: "To show that Science has a vital place in everyday life, that its achievements are transplanted at once into engineering practice and the industries, reducing arduous toil, promoting comfort, contentment, safety and general welfare."

Month by month, progress was slow, while blocks of Sears Roebuck and Co. stock from the original shares donated by Rosenwald were sold periodically to secure cash for construction and maintenance. For nearly a year the coal mine had to be shut down so that construction in the south hall could be continued, and this further decreased public interest and attendance. But by February 1939 enough prog-

ress had been made so that a special preview under the auspices of the Commercial Club could be announced for the
following April 14.

By this time the interior had been truly transformed. Extending around the central rotunda, now free of all the scaf-
folding, was an inscription suggested by Dawes; in bronze
letters more than two feet high it read: "SCIENCE DIS-
CERNS THE LAWS OF NATURE. INDUSTRY APPLIES
THEM TO THE NEEDS OF MAN." The major exhibit in
the rotunda, with four enormous marble-faced piers supporting its dome 120 feet above the floor, was the Periodic Table
of the Chemical Elements. At the main entrance to the north
court were two bronze, paneled doors, each with a weight of
nearly a ton and with thirteen panels bearing significant
figures, equations, instruments, machines, and legends to
represent the subjects within the scope of the Museum:
mathematics, measurement of space, measurement of time,
chemistry, medicine, physics, power, textiles and forestry,
architecture and civil engineering, transportation, geology
and mineral industries, communication, and graphic arts.
"The great doors," wrote Fox in *Notes*, "serve a dual purpose: portals to the building and to the thought within." On
the walls of the entrance vestibule were mounted bronze
plaques of Greek gods and goddesses typifying the sciences
and industries, from Apollo, as builder of cities, representing architecture and civil engineering, to Zeus, as father of
the deities, depicting the fundamental science of physics
and its application to power.

Into the four great halls, whose floors were now of marble and with large, simple, round columns supporting the
balconies above, exhibits were being moved. Historical locomotives and early automobiles went into the east hall,
with its balcony the site for models of airplanes and other
exhibits relating to aviation and planes of historical interest
suspended from the ceiling as if in flight. The long west hall
was for exhibits of power engines and displays of machines

of electric generation and transmission, and in the south hall
thus far only the headframe of the coal mine and the surrounding panels depicting the lore of coal making. In the
quadrants and stair towers were other large exhibits, among
them a giant printing press donated by the *Tribune,* a
ninety-ton steam stamp, a six-foot wedge gate valve, a steam
hammer, a modern automobile that, at the push of a button,
split apart to show the construction throughout its length
and the operation of its parts. On one side of the north hall
was a large room, two stories high, destined for special displays to be changed from time to time. The first balcony led
to a reference room and library above, with stacks for as
many as 175,000 volumes; there were rooms on the other
balconies for curators, administrators, and assorted executives, research laboratories, and the engineering department
and drafting room. In the basement were a photographic
studio, vaults, and a darkroom. Other features of the interior included two air-conditioned dining areas—a cafeteria
for 150 adults and a special children's lunchroom for a hundred—and a series of shops where models would be made and
exhibits built and maintained. True enough, a decade had
passed since reconstruction of the building was begun, wrote
Trent S. Sanford, curator of architecture and civil engineering, in *Notes,* but he took special note of what he described
as the "sunny side" of the interminable delays: "The result is,
without question, more successful than it would have been
some years ago. Further study has brought about a more
suitable interior; new materials and improved equipment
have brought about a more efficient interior; and the result is
an assembly of exhibits for a more valuable, more logical and
more attractive Museum."

There was little disagreement that Sanford was correct
in his estimate. But even as the preview was held and while
tribute in the handsome preview souvenir booklet once again
was paid to Julius Rosenwald ("He wanted to do something
important for the permanent cultural advantages of his city.

He felt that the organization of this Museum and its maintenance through the years would well serve the city and the people of Chicago"), and former Senator George Wharton Pepper of Pennsylvania, the keynote speaker, orated about the Museum and its exhibits as "the progeny of two newlyweds, science and industry, this happy pair," the exultation of the occasion was heavily tinged with foreboding and dark knowledge of existing problems and the prospect of more perilous ones.

CHAPTER V

PROGRESS—AND PROBLEMS

Although he was almost blind and generally in poor health when he became the full-time president of the Museum of Science and Industry, Rufus Dawes earnestly devoted himself to its present and future. He came there as often as possible, sometimes being guided through the partially built interior by Sterling Ruston, newly arrived at the Museum as a clerk. He concerned himself with matters large and small and was especially adept at settling arguments between staff members. And he constantly sought to clarify and define the Museum's basic reasons for existence.

He tended to disagree with those who designated the Museum primarily as an educational institution. This he considered too broad a designation; so to describe it, he wrote in a letter to Dr. William A. Pusey, an official of the National Science Research Council, "suggests troops of children and immature men and women hurrying through another museum." He opposed rather strongly the often expressed view of Waldemar Kaempffert before, during, and after the time he was director, that the Museum was obligated to associate with industrial progress the accompanying social effects. Two of Kaempffert's examples of his theory had been the elevator and the cotton gin: the first had led to the invention of the skyscraper, the skyscraper to congestion of population, and congestion of population to an entire brood of social ills, and the second to the revival of the declining institution of slavery and eventually the Civil War. Dawes believed that efforts by the Museum to make such definite links between inventions and social problems would seem to commit the institution to acrimonious disagreement. "In such controversy," he wrote to Pusey, "there is no reason to suppose that men trained in science or expert in the application of science to industry would have a greater authority than the ordinary politician. I feel there is great danger in this approach."

He corresponded regularly with Howard Hayward, president of Philadelphia's Franklin Institute, with Dr. Frank B. Jewett, the Bell Telephone Laboratories president, and with Samuel Karrer, chairman of the scientific advisory council of the Maryland Academy of Science in Baltimore. To each he asserted repeatedly that the Museum's over-all aim was to stimulate intellectual curiosity. Exhibits, he insisted, should be planned for the benefit of that part of the public that included youngsters coming into or having reached high school age and those who were interested in all phases of civilization. He also leaned rather heavily to making the Museum interesting and attractive to workers in industry. "I believe," he wrote to Jewett, "that it would be an activity from which we could have very active expectations of support from industrial corporations."

By the time of the 1939 preview, Dawes had so sorted out his thoughts that he could combine statements of previous years with his own to the point where he could formulate the inscription circling the central dome and enunciate what he considered a reasonable philosophic and pragmatic guide for the future: "It is the function of the Museum of Science and Industry to explain the methods whereby science discovers, genius invents and industry applies the facts and laws of nature to be used in the forward march of civilization. This it attempts to do not by static lifeless exhibits, but in living, moving demonstrations of precision, beauty and color. . . . The exhibits will stimulate the intellectual curiosity and bring the public to a better knowledge and understanding of the progress that has been made, and of the great improvement that may yet be attained in the living conditions of men by the cooperation of science and industry."

2.

Although he had resolved the philosophic problem to his meticulous satisfaction, matters far more immediate and vexatious plagued Dawes, and they were crucial to the Museum's very existence even as he and the trustees dared to hope to move ahead from the preview to an official full-scale opening in 1940. The plain truth was that, as the year was drawing to a close, the Museum was in its most precarious financial state. Construction costs and the expense of maintenance and operation had steadily depleted the capital established by Rosenwald's contributions. In the year starting in July 1938 the deficit amounted to $353,000 and could be made up only by selling more of the Sears Roebuck and Co. stock. This had been the pattern almost annually, and there now remained some twenty thousand shares, worth $1,200,-000.

At somber and depressing meetings the trustees pondered ways to cut costs and increase revenues. Should the free-admission policy be altered? The general conclusion was that attendance would surely be cut if a fee were charged on three days a week (studies of similar institutions showed that patronage fell by 65 per cent on non-free days), with a subsequent reduction in revenues from the coal mine and most certainly a diminution of total annual figures, which had to be high if industries were to be persuaded to spend many thousands of dollars on exhibits. Should an active drive be undertaken for corporate and individual memberships? This, too, was discarded, because the cost of such a campaign not only would put the Museum of Science and Industry in direct competition with both the Field Museum of Natural History and the Art Institute with many years' tradition of such public campaigns, but the cost of carrying it on might well be higher than probable receipts. Efforts in the state legislature to derive museum-tax revenues had failed several times, and a renewed attempt, even if success-ful—as it eventually was in 1941—would be of no help in the immediate crisis.

The Museum's plight was very much on Dawes's mind in the winter of 1939–40, and on one cold December day he re-layed the details—and more—to the man on whom he had relied so heavily for the success of A Century of Progress. At the end of the fair's second year, Lenox Lohr had moved to New York to become president of the National Broadcasting Company, but he retained, as a trustee, an active interest in the affairs of the Museum.

During his business trips to Chicago he always called on Dawes to talk about its present and future. On one such visit that mid-December he telephoned to Dawes to arrange a meeting, but the old man asked him to remain in his hotel room. "I want to talk confidentially to you there," he said.

At once, upon his arrival, Dawes delved deeply into the Museum's financial condition. He told how rapidly the Ro-senwald millions were being depleted, how little new in-come was in prospect. "Unless something radical is done," said Dawes, "the Museum will probably be out of funds in two years." Dawes had other complaints: He believed that various members of his staff were furnishing him with con-flicting reports and data on Museum operations, that his or-ders were being ignored or disobeyed, that at least two of the staff members were flagrantly disloyal.

Then he asked, "Can you take a leave of absence from NBC to see what you can do about straightening out this situation?"

This, said Lohr, was impossible because of the pressures of his job. But he did make a specific promise. "I'll be back next month and then I'll take some days off and look into things enough so that I can give you some suggestions."

3.

Before Lohr could make good that promise, Dawes, three weeks after the hotel-room conversation, was stricken with a fatal heart attack on January 8 in his Lake Shore Drive home. Trustees' meetings continued, as dismally as ever, with Colonel Sprague as temporary president. Again, consideration was given to charging admissions, seeking new members, striving for emergency legislation in Springfield, and, as an additional suggestion, even to close the Museum in the winter months. To study the problem intensively, a special ways-and-means committee was named, headed by Philip R. Clarke, conscientious president of the City National Bank and, as the civic-minded president of the Commercial Club, fully aware of the Museum's dilemma, and with Sewell Avery and George A. Ranney as members.

Clarke took his task with great seriousness. Almost nightly for three weeks after his appointment he held conferences with Fox and Frank C. Boggs, a retired Army colonel whom Dawes had brought with him from the lakefront fair to be the Museum's business manager. The sessions were as discouraging as they were lengthy. Fox and Boggs clung at first to their opinion that $410,000 was needed annually to operate the Museum adequately, but that with some curtailments—fewer curators and guides, limitation of visiting hours, alternate closing of certain portions—such expenses might be cut to $350,000. This, Boggs warned, was an absolute minimum. To go beneath it would make of the Museum what he called a "dead institution," with operations so impaired as to menace attendance and patronage of exhibits.

Instead of taking such drastic action, Clarke and Fox agreed
that it would be better to shut down completely. Extensive
explorations and discussions continued of existing—and possible—sources of income. The only assured source was about
sixty thousand dollars in dividends from the remaining
twenty thousand shares of stock and twenty thousand dollars from admissions to the coal mine. Corporate memberships *could* bring an additional twenty thousand dollars and
individual memberships twenty-five thousand dollars. A museum tax *could* yield $130,000. General admission charges
might be instituted, but the Museum's attorney, Willard
King, warned that to retain its right to museum-tax revenues,
the Museum would have to be free at least four days a week
and that resultant income from this source would amount to
about fifteen thousand a year. Mitchell McKeown, head of
the Community Fund, sat in on some of the meetings and
proposed soliciting large foundations; Fox was certain he
could enlist such financial help and subsequently visited
the more prominent among them, with uniformly unsuccessful results. Also considered as potential long-range sources
were annual contributions from the Commercial Club and
other civic organizations, a discreet campaign for bequests
from wealthy individuals to an official endowment fund,
further help from the Rosenwald Family Association, and
direct contributions from industry; on the latter, Clarke felt
that an appeal ought to be based on the contention that the
Museum was a perfect medium for promoting a better public
understanding of industry and consequently a friendlier attitude toward business.

Until the various matters were fully explored, Clarke proposed that any ceremonious opening be postponed and, most
importantly, that a permanent president be named as quickly
as possible to co-ordinate all activity. In a long report to
Sprague on February 21 detailing the variegated investigations and discussions of how to cut expenses and where to
seek needed income, he urged quick selection of "an able

Julius Rosenwald: His idea and multimillion-dollar gift led to the establishment of the Museum of Science & Industry.

The Palace of Fine Arts at the 1893 World's Columbian Exposition, described then as "unequaled since the Parthenon and the age of Pericles."

In the 1920s the noble structure was deserted and slowly deteriorating.

In a 1928 planning conference, Rosenwald (front right) meets with (left to right) Sewell L. Avery, then the Museum's president, attorney Leo F. Wormser, director Waldemar Kaempffert, and board member William R. Abbott.

Left, Otto Kreusser, the Museum's director at its official opening, in 1933.

Above, Philip H. Fox, the astronomer who succeeded Kreusser in 1937.

and energetic executive free to give same his undivided attention throughout the next few crucial months." One name immediately proposed was that of General Robert E. Wood, then reported to be divesting himself of some of his responsibilities as head of Sears Roebuck and Co., but this proved to be a false hope.

Instead, a chance meeting on a New York street helped to resolve the critical problem.

4.

In the midst of the many conferences and consultations, Clarke went to New York to attend a directors' meeting of the United States Steel Corporation. On his way to board the Twentieth Century Limited back to Chicago, he ran into Lenox Lohr near Grand Central Station. When Lohr expressed sorrow over the death of Dawes, Clarke replied, "It's too bad that he couldn't live to see the opening of the full Museum. We're still hoping to open this year, but we're facing, as you may know, quite a problem in devising ways and means of financing all our operations."

Lohr then told Clarke of the December meeting with Dawes in the hotel room and his promise to spend time trying to help ease the crisis. "That promise still holds. I'll always be interested in the welfare of anything with which Rufus Dawes was ever connected. Let me know if I can be of any help."

On the train that night, Clarke was struck with the thought that instead of having Lohr act as a consultant, he ought to be invited to become the Museum's new president. Clarke reflected on the great success Lohr had achieved as general manager of A Century of Progress, and he knew him to be a man with the ability to combine hardheaded business sense with a flair for real showmanship. Back in Chicago,

Clarke broached the idea to General Charles Dawes, who expressed hearty agreement.

Then began a series of meetings with Lohr during Clarke's business trips to New York. At the first, the banker again gave a résumé of the various problems at the Museum and emphasized the basic need for a strong successor to Dawes. "I think the presidency of that institution," he said, "would give the right man an exceptional opportunity to make an eminent place for himself in both science and industry." Two weeks later, the two men met again. Lohr expounded on the need for stimulating attendance at the Museum and of persuading major corporations that maintaining exhibits there was of inestimable public-relations value. The man who headed such an institution and devoted himself fully to it, said Lohr, would have to possess excellent administrative ability, set specific goals, be firm, make drastic changes that undoubtedly would engender criticism. But ultimately he would make the Museum a major success for all involved: exhibitors, participating industries, educators, scientists, and, above all, a vast and always growing public.

When Lohr finished his discourse, Clarke said, "I agree that we need a man of exceptional capacity and I know of only one man who has all of the qualifications, and that man is Lenox Lohr."

Before Lohr could reply, Clarke urged him not to discard the suggestion without considering the proposal fully and in all its aspects—not the least of which was the economic fact that the job would pay twenty-five thousand dollars a year, compared with the sixty thousand dollars Lohr was receiving as president of the radio network. "If you can adjust to that change," Clarke continued, "there are at least three considerations that I think would appeal to you. One is the great importance of the work itself. The second is your love for Chicago. And the third is the chance to carry on to conclusion the vision of your good friend, Rufus Dawes."

Lohr made no definite reply. "Let me give it some thought," he said.

Ten days later, at another meeting, Clarke pressed forward with his proposition. And as they departed with Lohr's assurance that he was still considering the offer, Clarke said, "Remember, Major, you'll leave your footprints more indelibly in the sands of time as president of the Museum of Science and Industry than a hundred presidents of the National Broadcasting Company."

CHAPTER VI

ENTER LENOX LOHR

The man who was being asked to assume the difficult task of saving the Museum of Science and Industry was a confirmed goal setter who analyzed situations and then drove forward to established ends. Precise and systematic, he advocated what he termed "an engineering approach" to problems; asked once for his criteria of success, he replied, "To work with your hands and ability and to see the result of that work—and get pleasure out of doing it." Then forty-eight, Lenox Lohr was brisk and sometimes brusque, short and slim, with bushy eyebrows and a bald head, and a record of success in four separate careers.

He was born on August 15, 1891, in Washington, D.C., where his father was a wholesale lumber dealer and his mother one of the first female lawyers in that city and an aide to Albert A. Michelson in his pre-Nobel laureate days as a physicist at the United States Naval Observatory. As a high school youth, Lohr was unusually inventive, at one time converting the gas-lit family home to electricity and during each summer buying an old automobile, repairing and restoring it, and then selling it at a profit. From Cornell University, where he was an honor student in mechanical and electrical engineering and served as a colonel of his cadet corps, he went almost at once into the Army and by a roundabout but determined way he managed to fulfill a desire to join the Corps of Engineers. This had been his original intention upon graduation in 1916, but at the time, Cornell and nine other selected schools each were allowed by the Army to name an honor graduate for direct commission in any branch except the Corps of Engineers. He accepted a commission in the Coast Artillery, but before he was called to duty he took and won a competitive examination for civilian engineers for Engineer Corps commissions. Because regulations forbade transfers from the Coast Artillery to the branch he yearned for, he stayed for six months, then resigned his first lieutenant's commission to re-enter as a second lieutenant of engineers. In overseas service in France as a captain he won a Silver Star for gallantry in the Meuse-Argonne. Determined to remain an Army career man after the war, he taught electrical engineering and international law at the Army Engineers' school at Fort Humphreys.

Early in 1922, while he was assigned as a military aide to the White House, one of his duties was to escort distinguished visitors to the shrine of the Unknown Soldier, then in the Capitol rotunda. One such visitor was Colonel Gilbert A. Youngberg of the Engineer Corps, who engaged him in conversation and learned about his engineering background. Lohr was soon assigned to the office of the Chief of Engineers, one of his tasks being to edit *The Military Engineer*, the bimonthly publication of the Society of American Military Engineers, of which Colonel Youngberg was president. The magazine was in bad shape, with precisely $92.50 in its bank account and five thousand dollars in debts, mostly for printing. Lohr settled in a small dimly lit office and advertised for a civilian editorial assistant. First to respond was Tennessee-born Martha McGrew, a perky young woman who had been working her way through George Washington University law school by selling life insurance. General A. Owen Seaman, for whom she had worked in the Motor Transport Corps during the war, had advised her, "Don't take that job. The magazine is on the rocks. They've pulled a colonel off as editor and put an unknown young captain in charge, because it won't make any difference if it folds." Despite the warning, Miss McGrew reported to the unknown young captain and told him what General Seaman had said. "C'mon, let's take it and fool them," was Lohr's reply.

With the $92.50 Miss McGrew bought stamps for letters soliciting subscriptions from a list of reserve Engineer Corps officers all over the United States. This yielded $450, which promptly went to pay off part of the publication's debts. Lohr was soon promoted to major, and month by month, year by year—with staff members whose ranks included such men destined for later fame in military and related fields as Leslie H. Groves, John C. H. Lee, Carl Gray, and Lucius Clay—the magazine managed to survive and prosper.

2.

One of the members of the editorial board of *The Military Engineer* was Colonel John Sewell, who had commanded the wartime regiment in which Charles G. Dawes had been a lieutenant colonel. Sewell and Dawes had maintained a close friendship after the war, while Sewell was president of the Alabama Marble Company and Dawes was engaged with his brother, Rufus, in organizing utilities firms before serving as Calvin Coolidge's vice-president. On frequent trips to Washington, Sewell visited the offices of *The Military Engineer* and came to know Lohr well.

In 1929, plans for A Century of Progress in Chicago had reached a point where Rufus Dawes, its president, required a general manager with proven administrative prowess and a capacity for withstanding pressures from politicians and businessmen seeking special favors. From Sewell came a suggestion: "I think Lohr would make you a good man." As president of *The Military Engineer* management board,

General Dawes was quite aware of what Lohr had done with the magazine, and he urged his brother to interview him. Lohr had already spent considerable time beyond his required tour of duty in Washington and was scheduled for transfer. He told Rufus Dawes that he had never been to a fair or exposition of any kind but that he had rather clearly defined ideas about management and about handling people. Dawes was impressed with the young major's direct, no-nonsense manner and his analytical approach, and promptly hired him.

3.

The exposition to celebrate Chicago's centennial observance of its official incorporation as a village in 1833 climaxed nearly a decade of discussion, setbacks, delays, renewals, and planning. Rufus Dawes had been among the first, back in 1923, to propose such an undertaking, and an organizing committee had been formed, disbanded, and re-formed with Dawes as its chairman and then as president of the entire project. The idea was to create on two man-made islands at the western edge of Lake Michigan a complex of scientific, cultural, industrial, and commercial buildings and exhibits. When the lakefront fair had first been conceived, the nation was still lush with postwar prosperity, but in the period between the time Lohr was named general manager and the scheduled opening in 1933, each month seemed less propitious for the staging of such an event. In Springfield, as in other state capitals, crowds of unemployed besieged the Illinois state legislature demanding relief. The state's coal fields were torn by war between rival labor factions. Court dockets were jammed with foreclosure suits and eviction cases. Samuel Insull's utility empire had collapsed, bringing added chaos and ruin to large and small investors. Hundreds of banks closed throughout the state, impoverishing thousands

more. Chicago's reputation had been sullied by the incessant
warfare between rival gangs and its carnage and bloodshed,
and the buffoonlike behavior of William Hale "Big Bill"
Thompson after he was elected mayor, for the third time, in
1927.

Yet the Dawes brothers and others involved in carrying
out the idea to its colorful fruition would not be dismayed.
They were determined to hold the exposition—and without
governmental subsidy or stock sales. On the eve of his departure as U.S. ambassador to Great Britain, General Dawes
set up a ten million dollar bond issue and made personal
visits to the city's top business and industrial leaders and issued a public statement throbbing with challenge and civic
pride and designed to loosen their corporate purse strings:
"There are no prophets of evil here who say that, not withstanding two years of hard work and steady progress in this
enterprise, this city, our pride, dear to us in having made
each one of us what we are, will lie down like a dog on its
back with its feet in the air and change its motto from 'I
Will' to 'I Surrender.' Let there be no mistake. We are not
less courageous than our forebears." Within twenty-four
hours, ten million dollars was pledged in bond-issue guaran-
tees.

One by one the elements in the conception began to take
form at the new Burnham Park and Northerly Island—the
Travel and Transport Building resembling a thousand-foot
ocean liner, the replicas of Fort Dearborn, Abraham Lin-
coln's log-cabin birthplace, and the 1860 Wigwam where he
won his first presidential nomination, the Hall of Science that
would be the dominant building of the fair, the bridge span-
ning the lagoon between the islands, the Social Science
Building, the Lama Temple, the reproduction of the Golden
Pavilion of Jehol, the Midway amusement area, the amazing
Sky Ride with twin towers sixty-four stories high and cables halfway down, from which were suspended rocket cars
whose riders could get a stupendous view of all the sights

below, dozens upon dozens of individual companies' buildings designed mainly along modern, geometrical lines—and on May 27, 1933, all was ready for what Rufus Dawes acclaimed as "the spontaneous expression of the pride of the citizenship of Chicago." As if to exemplify the basic theme of man's triumphs through his mastery of science and the exposition's slogan, "Application of science to industry," the fair's thousands of lights were set ablaze on opening night with energy captured from the rays of the star Arcturus, forty light-years, or 240 trillion miles, away.

As general manager, Lohr was extremely effective. He brought Martha McGrew with him as his administrative assistant, and she proved tireless in supervising myriad details and overseeing all aspects of the twenty-five million dollar enterprise ("She guards the interests of the World's Fair administration," wrote an interviewer, "with the sleeplessness of a watchdog"). An old Army associate, Colonel John Stewart, also came from Washington, and in subsequent months, Lohr gathered about him other Army-trained aides including John Sewell; Charles Walton Fitch, Lohr's childhood friend and wartime fellow officer, and Frank C. Boggs. Strict rules were set for all exhibitors. Other events of such magnitude had usually given free space to industries, but Lohr conceived—and successfully carried out—the practice of having the various companies pay not only the initial construction costs but fees for maintenance of the buildings that housed their exhibits. Each day, Lohr made two Army-style inspections of the three-mile-long exposition grounds from one end to the other. He was especially solicitous about the relationships with reporters assigned to cover the exposition. "They've got a job to do," he instructed Miss McGrew. "Help them to do that job. Never stand in their way. Don't tell them how to do it, and always be honest with them."

There were, of course, problems. The most vexing one resulted from Sally Rand's dance performances in the "Streets of Paris" in the nude except for two frilly ostrich-feather fans, a feat that resulted in her arrest several times but created for the former Midwest farm girl a new career that endured for many years. And there were inevitable grumbles about establishment of an 11:30 P.M. curfew for admissions and occasional complaints from concessionaires on the Midway.

But over-all results were impressive. "There were no holdups, no embezzlements," Lohr later wrote in *Fair Management*, his book detailing plans, procedures, and methods of operation of the massive exposition. "No forgeries; no pestilence; no counterfeiting of tickets; no strikes other than jurisdictional; no lawsuits deriving from contractual relations; no claims by contractors for extension of time; no political interference; no structural failures; and no catastrophes." For all the publicity about Sally Rand and other dancers who quickly adopted her terpsichorean innovations, those who had set the theme for the fair were satisfied that vast numbers of the public had found the scientific aspects fascinating, instructive, and, because of the graphic manner in which most of the exhibits had been designed, vastly entertaining. Even on days when general attendance was slack, the aisles of the Hall of Science were invariably jammed, with visitors five deep around the geological time clock or studying lessons in electromagnetism or listening to lectures on mathematics.

Beyond the qualitative triumph, the exposition proved remarkable in another respect: it was a financial success, with total gate receipts of $10,345,848 and concessionaires' grosses of $26,084,777. By the end of the second season, revenues were enough so that all bondholders were paid, all expenses were accounted for, and, according to prearrangements, remaining profits of $160,000 after payments for demolition were divided among beneficiaries ranging from the Museum of Science and Industry ($40,000) and the Art Institute ($32,000) to the Association for the Perpetuation of Fort Dearborn ($8,000) and the Chicago Regional Planning Commission ($6,400).

When checks to these recipients were distributed, editorialists took proper note of the remarkable fact that this was the first time in history that any exposition of major stature had ended without a deficit, a result especially notable for having been achieved in the midst of a world-wide depression. "For any business to make money in 1933 and 1934 was unusual," stated the Chicago *Times*. "For a brand new business in a line of endeavor that had previously never produced a profit-maker to wind up those two years with a surplus was phenomenal. . . . Too much credit for this grand finale cannot be given to Rufus C. Dawes, nor to Lenox Lohr. But all Chicago shares in the credit. Without splendid cooperation all along the line, the fair could never have made the record it did. We can't be very pessimistic over the future of a city with the spirit that did that. Such people can't be kept down long."

4.

For a time Mayor Kelly spoke enthusiastically of the economic benefits the exposition had brought to the city and proposed making it a permanent attraction. He announced that he hoped to obtain thirteen million dollars either from the Works Progress Administration or the Public Works Administration and that Lohr was unquestionably his choice to be general manager. But plans for such an undertaking languished and perished, and in Christmas week of 1935 Lohr accepted an offer to become president of the National Broadcasting Company after turning down a proposal to run the huge New York World's Fair scheduled for 1939.

Lohr assumed his new job early that January, succeeding Merlin H. Aylesworth, who became chairman of the parent Radio Corporation of America's movie subsidiary, the Radio-

Keith-Orpheum Corporation. He brought with him, among others, Martha McGrew as assistant and Fitch as business manager of the program department.

Lohr was admittedly without experience in radio; he had four sets in his Evanston home during his term as the fair's general manager, but he admitted to a *Newsweek* interviewer that he had seldom listened to them. The magazine also dutifully recorded his entertainment preferences: "I like good, light music, especially musical comedies with a point to them like 'Roberta' and 'Naughty Marietta.' I like thoughtful drama and speeches that entertain as well as educate."

From the start of his NBC presidency, Lohr was intrigued by the prospects for television, then in its infancy. "It is safe to say," he declared in a 1937 speech, "that in time the public will have paraded before it programs of a variety and scope of entertainment and education beyond that which any other entertainment medium has been able to offer." In his periodic reports he urged constant development of the new medium and increases in expenditures for research and sale of sets. In 1938, when the network televised Gertrude Lawrence performing in a scene from her current Broadway hit *Susan and God,* Lohr was quick to predict—at a time when the watchword among theater men was "No concessions to television!"—an entirely new kind of drama especially written for television cameras far more complex and versatile than the one used for the experimental telecast. He spoke often on the public responsibilities of radio, on the need for more rigid controls over excessive gunplay and violence in programs aimed at children, on the rights of radio and other media to freedom of expression. He hired James Rowland Angell, former president of Yale University, to be the network's educational counselor and enthusiastically backed appropriations for the formation of what came to be the internationally renowned NBC Symphony under the direction of Arturo Toscanini and Artur Rodzinski, a cycle of

Shakespeare's plays starring John Barrymore, and a series of dramas by Eugene O'Neill.

Meanwhile he was successfully supervising the revamping of the network, strengthening relationships with its station outlets, and establishing a sounder financial base for future operation. In the New York *Times*'s annual review of the industry at the end of 1939, he reported increases in income over 1938 and foresaw, on the basis of contracts signed, greater revenues for 1940. And he was bullish about television: "The new year finds television an accomplished, even if limited service. We shall leave no stone unturned to put on programs that people want to see badly enough to buy receiving sets."

5.

Now, in the spring of 1940, after having proved himself in three diversified careers—as editor of *The Military Engineer*, as general manager of A Century of Progress, and as president of the National Broadcasting Company—Lohr pondered the invitation from Philip Clarke to take on a fourth that promised strife and difficulties, challenges and satisfactions.

As he considered Clarke's offer, he was moved by the chance to bring order out of obvious chaos at the institution that his friend and mentor, Rufus Dawes, had attempted to lead at the time of his death. Moreover, he had enjoyed his years in Chicago and the friends he had made. "It's the only place," he told Miss McGrew, "where I felt I belonged to the community. Chicago has been awfully good to me. Nobody ever heard of me before the fair. Chicago took me in and gave me a chance. This is a chance to repay that city for what it did for me." And because he was enough of an egotist to enjoy public recognition for tasks begun and accomplished, he was impressed by Clarke's counsel that he could make his life count for a good deal more as head of the Museum of Science and Industry than as president of a radio network, however vast and powerful. The difference in salary—twenty-five thousand dollars as against sixty thousand—was insignificant, because Mrs. Lohr had inherited property and he himself had made profitable investments.

By May, Lohr was close to a decision. On May 16 he lunched at the Chicago Club with Clarke, Sprague, Ranney, and Avery. There was conversation about the war in Europe and President Roosevelt's forthcoming bid for a third term, and then, toward the end of the meeting, Clarke said, "Lenox, I have been officially authorized by the board to offer you the presidency of the Museum."

Lohr asked for a little more time, but as he and Clarke walked out of the building he told the banker, "Phil, I've just about made up my mind to take it but I need a week or so to wind things up there."

On June 7 Lohr telephoned Clarke from New York: "OK, I accept. Pass the word."

CHAPTER VII

FROM THE BRINK OF EXTINCTION

The public announcements were made; the formalities of officially notifying the board of Lohr's decision were swiftly carried out. Within a week Lohr was in Chicago, having paused in Philadelphia for two days to talk to officials and staff members of the Franklin Institute. He began at once a series of conferences with a variety of people, including William and Lessing Rosenwald, and most especially with Frank Boggs, his one-time associate at the exposition and now business manager.

As a Museum trustee, Lohr had been cognizant not only of growing financial problems but of what he considered a prime contributing factor: the traditional organization of the Museum into departments whose curators bore full responsibility for every aspect of their respective subject areas. He had respect for the curators' scientific and intellectual status and academic accomplishments, but he definitely believed that the conventional system made for inflexibility and produced operating costs that would remain high so long as each curator assembled his exhibits piecemeal, partly by machines and models constructed in the Museum's workshop and partly with isolated objects, antiques, and historical items acquired from industry or private sources, some of which were still stored in warehouses. Not only was a good part of a curator's time spent in basic research and designing exhibits, but he was also expected to write explanatory copy for labels and pamphlets, devise lighting, and supervise half a dozen other activities in the department or pay to have these extra tasks carried out.

It was obvious to Lohr that not enough money was going to be available for even a small percentage of the planned exhibits and that this diffuse arrangement created difficulties in co-ordinating over-all operations and added considerably to the existing financial burden. Moreover, there was intense competition among the various curators for space and for what money was available, because each quite naturally felt that his field of interest was more important than any other. What Lohr had learned at past meetings and from Dawes and conversations with other trustees and from his informal survey of the existing status of exhibits was sufficient to persuade him at the advent of his presidency that he had to make his first important move in this area, even before spelling out any changes in the basic philosophy of the Museum's operation.

2.

The summer was destined to be hot, long, and acrimonious.

On July 8, Lohr visited the Museum for a brief meeting with Fox, curators, and key members of the staff. The tone was genial, but Lohr, in a brief talk, avowed that he intended to be a very active president and would be in close touch with all of them. Two days later, Fox received a letter from Boggs suggesting that in view of Lohr's undoubted intention to assume many of the director's duties in reorganizing the Museum, he might consider resigning. Fox insisted that only the trustees could ask for his resignation, but his protest availed him little.

Lohr had asked each of the eighteen curators for reports on current progress and projected expenses in their departments. He pored over these and held more meetings with Boggs, and on August 2 sent to six of them and to six other staff members letters that began, "It is a source of keen regret to me that my first communication with you has to be an unpleasant one." He went on to explain the need to reduce expenditures and to inform each that with termination of their services would go two extra weeks' salary, payment for accumulated leave, a month's pay for every year worked, and the privilege of using existing offices and the Museum's secretarial facilities for seeking new affiliations. Curators dismissed were F. C. Brown, physics; Robert Moulton, chemistry; J. A. Folse, power; R. B. May, transportation; Trent Sanford, architecture and civil engineering; and Helmuth Bay, forestry. Others who received Lohr's letter included John Maloney, librarian Mary B. Day, and Erik Fenger, staff engineer and electrician.

In addition, seven others, primarily secretarial and clerical employees in the departments affected, were also given dismissal notices. Almost without exception, all found new positions of equal or higher rank shortly after they left the Museum, but bitterness was inevitable.

Fox made one final major effort to thwart Lohr. On August 22, he sent to each trustee a lengthy document covering in detail the conditions under which he had been hired in 1937, his efforts to carry out the mandate to create a network of exhibits that "should show primarily the dependence of our modern civilization on science and on its application in industry," the progress toward completion of construction, and a revised budget of $275,000, considerably lower than earlier estimates. He included the correspondence from Boggs and an account of his parley with Lohr and his evaluations of each person discharged, and, implying that Lohr had been influenced by Boggs in designating those to be dismissed, wrote, "If one were to look for the person who served as an analogy for Madame Defarge of the Reign of Terror, he would not have far to seek." He invited the trustees to "construe this statement as a resignation" if they felt that he was no longer needed as director. And he reserved his strongest, most emotional terms for Lohr: "What has taken place in your Museum in these first days of Mr. Lohr's presidency is an assault without parallel and without precedent in any American cultural institution. It is an affront to the intelligence of the community. It has started unfavorable comment in the scientific world; it has been termed a 'blitzkrieg,' 'putsch' and 'Naziism.' . . . If this dictatorial action can be tolerated in this Museum of Thought, in whose founder's character the keynote was the recognition of human values, what hope is there for American institutions in general? Ruthlessness cannot in any guise be construed as a virtue."

Four days later, Fox's statement was read in full at a trustees' meeting. Defending the moves he had taken, Lohr declared, "I made no snap judgments about these dismissals and Dr. Fox's. I gave it all very careful consideration. It's imperative that it be done to reduce expenses." Thereupon the trustees voted to accept Fox's resignation and passed a resolution giving him seven months' salary and expressing "appreciation for the energetic manner in which he has carried forward the work of preparing the building and exhibits to their present state of completion."

The clamor was only partially stilled. Ralph Gerard, the famed University of Chicago physiologist and president of the local chapter of the American Association of Scientific Workers, named a committee of two university colleagues, the equally renowned Anton J. Carlson and Arthur Holly Compton, and Charles H. Behre, Jr., a Northwestern University geologist, to make a formal inquiry into the dismissal of their fellow scientists. Fox promptly released copies of his eight-page document to the local newspapers and wire services and the influential *Science* magazine. *Time* magazine, among others, took note of the event in a story headed "Oomph for Science" that stressed Lohr's intentions to hew more closely to the theory that the Museum be a medium for mass education rather than a static repository with strong academic underpinning. Despite the publicity, only five letters from the general public reached Lohr's desk, three of them commending him for "getting rid of the deadwood" and two criticizing him.

3.

The furor soon subsided and Lohr continued to concentrate on other matters.

At his first board meeting as president, he told the trustees that he would give priority to increasing the number of Museum visitors considerably. In 1939 the attendance had been 470,306, and prospects were that 1940's figure would be slightly more than five hundred thousand. Lohr's aim was to attract one million annually as soon as possible and not only to keep attendance at that level but to continue to add to it year after year. He considered that the success of the Museum could be measured by the attendance in the same way that the success of a corporation could be shown by its profit statements. With greater attendance, he would be able more effectively to persuade industrial companies to build and maintain at space rates expensive exhibits based, as in radio, on a reasonable and equitable return in terms of cost per thousand visitors. And he vowed to undertake a concentrated program of seeking the co-operation of industry as a prime means of gaining financial support for the Museum. The hoped-for one-million-attendance mark and establishment of a sound principle of greater industrial participation were among twenty-eight objectives he set out for the board, a list that served him well as a guide in ensuing years as, one by one, they were nearly all attained. Among these aims were to open the main section to the public before the year was out, to balance the operating budget, to establish the Museum more firmly as a prime Chicago asset, to produce guidebooks, tour materials, and other printed matter for visitors' benefit, to restyle and redecorate most of the sections, to secure a proper balance of exhibits including various unrepresented fields, to expand systematic tours by school children and encourage tours by adult organizations, to secure scientific and educational recognition by enlisting the services of eminent scientists and educators on the board of trustees and on science advisory committees, to complete landscaping around the Museum, to survey all exhibit material so as to assure integrity and accuracy, to eliminate blatant advertising, product display, and trade-fair techniques, and to study the desires, habits, and requirements of visitors so that, as he expressed it, "a friendly rather than impersonal feeling will develop, by considering the public as invited guests and the staff as gracious hosts."

On another level, he moved to undo whatever damage Fox's allegations had created in the academic community. He invited Carlson and Compton to visit him at the Museum and laid out in detail all figures and statistics relating to costs, income both real and potential, and plans for the future. After an hour, the burly Carlson rose, jammed his hat on his close-cropped, steel-gray hair, and rumbled, "Well, I can see now that you did what you had to do." Compton, who had expressed apprehension earlier that the city's cultural life had been adversely affected by Fox's dismissal, made no immediate comment but promised to be patient and watchful; within four months he would agree to become a Museum trustee and join the other committee members in drawing up a statement about their investigation of the Fox case in which, although deploring the application of business standards rather than principles of academic tenure in the dismissals and subsequent methods of remuneration, they expressed optimism about the Lohr regime. "Your committee," they stated, "is pleased to observe that the policy expressed by the president of the Museum is to continue emphasis on education rather than on entertainment."

At the end of the hectic summer, Lohr made his first public speech as president—appropriately, to the Commercial Club. He traced the Museum's origins and history, paid proper tribute to Rufus Dawes, described such projects under construction as a vast Santa Fe Railway model and a plasticized "transparent woman," and then struck at the core of the Museum's money problems. "We have been living largely on our fat, we have been using up our capital," he said. He cited annual income of eighty-five thousand dollars, primarily in dividends from Sears Roebuck and Co. stock, the four-hundred-thousand-dollar cost of operations, and the $375,000 on hand in cash. He itemized the steps he had taken in reducing the budget by over one hundred thousand dollars, adding, "Despite what you may have heard, only about twenty-five thousand dollars of that affected the curators." Replying to those who feared he would turn the Museum into another World's Fair, he said, "I know world's fair technique and I know trade fair technique, and none of it has any place in the Museum." Indeed, he added, there was already much in the Museum that was garish, in bad taste, or exemplified direct advertising, and as soon as possible, he promised, all this would be removed. He hoped to bring life and vitality to the Museum ("We'll dress it up. . . . The very nature of science and industry is romance and drama and action") and to show vividly the interrelationships of pure science, invention, applied science, and mass distribution by industry. Industries would be urged to develop and display exhibits that would trace sequences of scientific and industrial development from the scientific foundation through the first invention on through the development up to its most recent applications. Lohr also enlarged on a constant theme enunciated by some of his predecessors: "The Museum should be like a looseleaf encyclopedia and no exhibit ever finished. When a piece of machinery or process becomes obsolete, it should be taken out and the very latest development put in its place. It is very important that we stand on the premise that the exhibits in the Museum shall represent the latest, and that exhibiting industries feel a continuing proprietary interest and a definite responsibility to show not only what is the last word but perhaps a glimpse into what may be the last word of tomorrow." He noted the apparent lack of general public interest in the controversy swirling around the dismissal of Fox and the others ("If one-fifth that much publicity had been published about the World's Fair, we would have had a thousand letters, and at NBC one comment might bring forth a hundred thousand letters") and added, "We have to make this Museum live and be real in the heart of everyone in Chicago and an institution that will be a great national Museum, a show, in which science and industry will live as dramatic things." Underscoring the specific purposes of the Museum, he concluded, would be an additional goal: "In these days, when old standards are falling, when traditions are being looked at askance and new ideologies are creeping in, we can show that the American way of life and our high standard of living arose in a land of free enterprise and untrammeled minds, where the scientists could study and create, where there was a profit motive, if you wish, for the inventor to invent something, where the applied scientist could make a good living out of his work and where industry could make a profit. . . . We can demonstrate that not one per cent of our scientific achievements is perverted to the destruction of men and that science produces new industries which put far more men to work than are displaced. If we can do that, then we will make a very material contribution to society."

CHAPTER VIII

"TELL NOTHING

BUT THE TRUTH . . ."

At the Museum itself, much needed to be done if, as Lohr had promised, there would be a fullscale opening before the year was out. He was a late riser and rarely came to his office earlier than ten o'clock, but once there he concentrated deeply on what lay ahead. On the ride from his fourteen-room home in Evanston, he always directed his driver never to go more than forty miles an hour. "There is something about the movement and jiggling of the car at that speed," he once told Willard L. King, "that enables me, riding there, to be absorbed in problems and to think of things I don't think of elsewhere." He used this time to jot down ideas and notes and even likely phrases to be used in speeches. At his desk, Lohr would light the first of dozens of cigarettes for the day, summon a secretarial aide, usually Jennie Joos, and rapidly begin to dictate at once not only from his scribblings but also from excerpts gathered for him mostly by Martha McGrew—who had joined him at his new post—from material relating to the general subjects of museums, science, industry, theories of exhibits, and the like. Once typed, these were put into folders for handy reference. A typical listing of such notes read:

Exhibits must tell a story.

Science not to invent engines of destruction or machines to throw men out of work.

Laboratories full of new discoveries.

Ten years from conception to general public acceptance—television development.

Industry showed profit.

Live rather than static or historical exhibits.

Chicago trustee for national collection. Will profit in reputation, prestige and tourist dollars.

Conception should be of national institution.

Extracurricular activities should be as important as exhibits in building into the hearts and consciousness of Chicago.

People must get in habit of thinking about and coming to Museum.

Chicago did a great deal for me. I can repay that debt here.

Youth of today more interested in tomorrow than yesterday.

Statue of Liberty comes third.

Chicago a cross-roads.

Must be of value to manufacturers. Like a country, a corporation wants to show the new things it has to sell, not its dead antiques.

Incomplete Museum is like unfinished Fair.

Get it filled and perfect and eliminate afterwards.

Accolade to be exhibitor.

Exhibits should be designed for the public and not for the curator.

Sports and hobbies have large public appeal.

The mind of a man is less perturbed by a mystery that he cannot explain than by an explanation he cannot understand.

The wording of a sign should not be designed
to impress the erudite but to enlighten the visitor.

A woman can be beautiful and gay, and still be
dignified and virtuous.

The final comment recurred frequently, for Lohr was determined to apply some of the decorative principles that he
had learned from his experience at A Century of Progress. After a survey of existing exhibits and those nearing completion,
he curtly ordered a number of them shut down until they
could be redesigned and refashioned. One of the largest of
these was the agricultural section, on which Russell H. Anderson had spent nearly two years and which was virtually
ready, with thousands of agricultural devices and implements that had been gathered from farms everywhere, about
75 per cent of them primarily of historical interest.

Lohr disliked the kinds of cases that had been built in
the Museum shop to house the various items—unattractive
boxlike structures covered with beaverboard and institutional brown and tan like the surrounding walls. One of the
few sections that met with Lohr's approving eye was the
graphic arts department, where Daniel MacMaster, its assistant curator, had persuaded Fox to allow him to make
use of colors other than the traditional brown-tan combination. As for others, "We are not going to open that way,"
insisted Lohr. "It's all too drab and monotonous."

To bring about the changes he wanted, he summoned
ebullient Nathaniel Owings, a young architect from Cornell
University who had worked in the lakefront exposition's first
year as an aide to his brother-in-law, Louis Skidmore, director of design and construction, and Shep Vogel-gesang, a
color expert, and later as director of concessions. Since their
days at the fair, Skidmore and Owings had formed a fast-
rising architectural firm that would eventually be responsible for some of the country's mightiest—and aesthetically
advanced—buildings. Owings invaded the Museum with

Charles Dornbusch, his chief designer, and his corps of color and lighting experts, and they soon set about repainting walls in varieties of blues, reds, grays, and chalk-white to create a gayer and more festive atmosphere. And with the new paint motifs came floor coverings, usually of tile, whose colors harmonized with a section's over-all decorative plan.

2.

While these physical changes were being wrought, Lohr instituted a series of Friday meetings with staff members after the 4:30 P.M. closing hour—"very informal family talks," he called them. Attendance was not obligatory, as he replied to one man who wanted to know if extra compensation would be forthcoming. But he hoped that most would be present, because, as he said at the initial session, "There are so many ramifications in an institution of this kind that we are going to require the brains of each one of you and that means an understanding of our problems if we are all going to give material help to the solving of these problems." At the same meeting, he encouraged questions and vowed to be frank and direct in replying to all matters that concerned the Museum. "There are always rumors in our organization, many of them utterly without foundation, and yet they come apparently from good sources. Many of these you hear, but when we have these meetings, have no fear of asking any question that is on your mind. If you ask, 'When am I going to get a raise?' I may say, 'I don't know,' but you'll get an answer!"

He was near-evangelistic in espousing the purpose of the Museum as an effective medium of mass education as contrasted with formal education. The former he described as a process in which "to tell its story to instruct large unrelated groups and hold attention by intrinsic merit rather

than by personal guidance and individual attention in class-
rooms, all the devices of showmanship, curiosity, and entertainment must be used to intrigue initial interest, excite
curiosity, and offer explanations or demonstrations so lucid
and understandable that the student feels a compelling urge
to follow them through." Lohr emphasized the importance
of diligently carrying out assigned duties. It was incumbent
on him and on those in charge of exhibits not only to hold
visitors' attention from instant to instant but to build an
eager desire to come back again. As for the role of the
young demonstrators, Lohr reminded them of the favorable
comments about guides at A Century of Progress. "We have
the same problem here. The responsibility for the success
of the Museum is to a very large measure in the hands of
the demonstrators. You must be alert, aim to please the
public, make a favorable impression by manners and appearance. If you do not know the answer to a question,
admit it and ask the visitor to wait while you go and find
out. Remember, you are our host to the public." He urged
everyone to participate in engendering much more publicity
for the Museum to stimulate attendance. Everyone, he advised, should consider himself an "unofficial salesman" for
the Museum and be on the alert for stories and anecdotes
to be passed on to Miss McGrew for possible press releases.

And he was especially frank and detailed in apprising
his listeners of the Museum's financial condition at the time
he arrived and the reasons for taking the measures he felt
were crucially essential for the Museum's survival. He had
instituted economies, he declared, with two basic thoughts:
"To make cuts without fear or favor and not to make a cut
where the public would be affected." To meet an operating
budget for 1940 of $314,000 there was only eighty-five thou-
sand dollars, but this financial distress would be alleviated
somewhat, he noted, when, at the end of 1941, $120,000
would come from the amended museum-tax law. He disclosed, too, that William and Lessing Rosenwald had told

him they would approve further allotments from the Rosenwald Family Association only if the Museum were to
strengthen itself by closing considerably the gap between
income and expenditures. "That means that every particle
of income that we can get is absolutely essential. I propose
to put this thing in a position where there is no chance of
the Museum being closed. Very large sums of additional
money must be obtained, and the only place I see to get
them is from industry."

Response to these sessions was uniformly favorable. Many
who had experienced sagging morale after the dismissal
of Fox and the others were buoyed by Lohr's open-minded
approach and honest appraisals. All were impressed when,
at the end of one session in which he expounded on his
plans to enlist the co-operation of the giants of American
industry, Lohr declared, "I am going to take the responsibility here for anything that goes wrong. No matter how
much I may jump on you, it is my fault. There is nothing
wrong but what it is my fault. All I can do is to transmit to
you enough responsibility and hope that you will fulfill it
and you will transmit it on to others and hope they will
fulfill it."

3.

As he so often indicated in comments both formal and
informal during this period of reorganization and austerity,
Lohr considered widespread participation of industry of
paramount importance to the Museum. He earnestly sought
to convince executives of major companies whose co-operation he sought that good-will benefits were to be derived
from exposure of their companies in the Museum. This kind
of institutional public relations, he asserted, would yield
innumerable values to exhibiting firms. "If we do our part
right," he said, "we have a chance to sell industries to the

American people. For when we tell a story the public will believe us. We must tell no white lies. We must tell nothing but the truth. If we do this, there are dozens of things we can tell here for industry and make it worth while for industry to help us."

To aid in this vital undertaking, Lohr brought to the Museum two men who had served him well previously: Charles Walton Fitch, who had gone with him from A Century of Progress to the National Broadcasting Company as business manager for John Royal, the program director, and Paul M. Massmann, a debonair, Chicago-born salesman who also had served at the lakefront fair and then had prospered as an NBC radio-network time salesman. Fitch was named business manager after Colonel Boggs was called to active Army duty in November 1940, and Massmann, who prided himself on his expertise in salesmanship, was named manager of industrial exhibits and urged to use his powers of persuasion on heads of industrial corporations and follow through with co-operating firms in organizing and opening exhibits.

Lohr acknowledged the accomplishments at the institute's progenitor, the Deutsches Museum, but he wanted to reverse the emphasis. In the Munich museum, as in most of the early exhibits at the Museum of Science and Industry, as much as 90 per cent of the space was devoted to tracing historical development up to modern times. Lohr's concept was to switch proportions: 10 per cent devoted to the past and 90 per cent to the present. He felt not only that there would be much greater public interest in modern aspects of whatever products a specific industry chose to display but that most industries would be more likely to invest many hundreds of thousands of dollars in exhibits that showed the latest processes or products. One other basic belief of Lohr's was that at least 10 per cent of the Museum's total exhibits should be changed each year to keep abreast of current developments. Theoretically, this would create practically a new Museum every decade, and with annual changes there would be ample reason for visitors to return again and again.

For the guidance of prospective exhibitors, rules, suggestions, and the elements of Lohr's exhibit philosophy were formulated and incorporated into a manual. These grew out of valuable information he had acquired in his two years at A Century of Progress, from a study of other museums, and from practical application to one of the Museum's oldest exhibits, that of the Bell Telephone System. In the six years since this and other exhibits had been transferred in their entirety from the lakefront fair, much of the equipment had become inoperative because of a lack of personnel to make repairs. Lohr's relationship with the telephone company executives was a warm one, dating back to the years when he signed up the firm as the first commercial exhibitor at the 1933–34 fair. He now proposed that they take over the space for the exhibit, install modern equipment and assume responsibility and the cost of maintaining it. In exchange, an appropriate label, with clear, readable text, would be affixed to a prominent place in the exhibit indicating its sponsorship. Instead of a single curator determining the content of the exhibit, experts from the scientific staffs of the phone company and its affiliated firms, Western Electric and Bell Laboratories, would devise the entire display, emphasizing the modern and most recent techniques and, wherever feasible, prospects and inventions of the future.

An essential part of this proposal and those to all exhibitors was a contract guaranteeing that the exhibit would remain for five years, with a five-year extension if mutually agreed upon. This would assure each exhibitor an ample opportunity to amortize the original investment and the Museum the option of removing the exhibit at the end of five years if it were not properly maintained and kept up to date.

The company would pay the cost of building and installing its exhibit and be charged a fixed fee that would reimburse the Museum for all expenses incurred in operating, maintaining, and demonstrating it. This fee was not a rental based on the amount of space occupied but only on the actual cost of operation to the Museum. It would be paid once each year, without change, for the lifetime of the contract, thereby assuring the exhibitor that no unexpected bills would be presented for performance of minor services, and for it the Museum also would furnish all utilities, insurance, janitor service, and replacement and repair of broken or worn-out parts that did not require special skills of the exhibitors' own technicians and industrial experts. Also covered by the fee would be the cost of demonstrators' salaries.

Lohr early established the policy that all demonstrations be performed by Museum personnel rather than an exhibitor's employees. This would preclude any attempts of a sponsor to advertise directly, tout its products, or indirectly solicit patronage. Demonstrators were trained to explain only technical features and mechanics, and were prohibited from answering questions about prices or relative technical merits.

Enlarging on notes he dictated at his desk, Lohr wrote in the manual, "Exhibits should tell a logical and sequential story. They should begin with the most basic principle and, step by step, lead to the finished product. The exhibit sequence should show first what the public wants to see, then those things which the exhibitor thinks it ought to see. . . . The most technical of demonstrations will be understood by groups of different educational backgrounds if the consecutive steps in its development are logically presented. General interest is best reached when the individual can see an application to his own life or welfare."

Exhibitors were advised to create sequences with elements of dramatic and emotional appeal as well as the fundamentals of basic sciences. Each exhibit was to be an architectural entity and different in design from adjoining exhibits, thereby "giving a change of pace and delineating the area." Public participation was essential ("The public desires to use muscles and brain") and so was ample space for demonstrations to groups of at least thirty-five school children. Wherever possible, diversified techniques were to be used, for "in general, the public will not sit more than a few minutes without something to hold its attention, nor stand for more than 10 minutes even for something of high attraction," and while motion of itself was not essential, it was suggested as a most effective way to tell a story.

No fewer than forty-four exhibition techniques were listed, ranging from a diorama and various sizes of models to microscopic slides, comic strips, and question-and-answer boards. Labels and descriptive legends could be printed, hand-lettered, cast in bronze or plaster, etched in glass or plastic, engraved in plaster, wood, metal, or plastic, or cut from a variety of materials and applied to any surface in the form of cutout letters. Directions were included for everything from the most effective lighting ("In general, the best practice is to avoid general room illumination and to apply the light in generous quantities only where it is needed") to selection of best materials for exhibit construction and installation of electrical, heating, ventilation, and refrigeration systems.

Above all, Lohr insisted on a policy of complete honesty with all exhibitors. No roseate promises would be made that had scant hope of fulfillment. No favoritism would be shown to exhibitors with huge amounts to spend but small inclination to abide by the rules. In Lohr's view, for a firm to be represented in the Museum was an accolade and an honor. For its part, the Museum would strive for the loftiest of aims: "We have but one thing to sell—the truth and the eternal verities. Without political bias or a profit motive, it can demonstrate to its millions of visitors those fundamentals which have made America what it is."

4.

In conjunction with rules for prospective exhibitors, Lohr established several basic ones for staff members. One of the first was that only those articles, large or small, should be purchased for which funds were available. When it proved difficult to hire demonstrators and other floor personnel at the low salaries provided for in the budget, Lohr advised, "Just keep on hunting. You'll have to." He saw himself, as he said at one of the weekly staff meetings, "as the paid trustee, paid to protect the Museum's money," and he did not intend to violate by loose spending the trust that had been put in him. To underscore his perennial assertion that the public was paramount, he directed that no employee park his car in front of the building in spaces provided for visitors; he parked his own car at the rear and he encouraged others to do likewise.

Although he set up rules for exhibitors and personnel, Lohr was loath to impose more than rudimentary ones on visitors. "Let's not make too many rules for them," he counseled, "because these people are our life's blood." He worked excessively hard in these early months not only to insure a reasonably successful new opening in October, but because he was eager to begin molding a strong organization that would remove from him the burdens of the detailed, routine operations of the Museum and give him time for what he considered the creative aspects of his role. "My job involves creativity," he often told Willard King, "and creativity is a peculiar thing. It involves having ideas that no one else has thought of." He appeared to view what he had to do almost in terms of a military campaign, determined that here, as in the assignments given him in the Army, at A Century of Progress, and at the National Broadcasting Company, he would emerge the victor.

CHAPTER IX

CONQUERING A CRISIS

When the full central pavilion was formally opened in October 1940, there were a number of new exhibits to intrigue visitors, including an array of modern printing equipment and a press donated by the *Tribune,* a full-sized iron foundry, and a million-volt Westinghouse surge generator capable of demonstrating man-made lightning. But the undoubted hit was the Santa Fe Railway's one hundred thousand dollar, three thousand-square-foot model system depicting its transcontinental operations over the grainfields of the Middle West, the cotton, oil, and cattle-grazing fields of the South and Southwest, the Grand Canyon, the Rocky Mountains, and California's Imperial Valley. Destined to be a popular attraction for many years to come, it had taken six months to construct the model from five tons of plaster, with half a ton of coloring for scenic effects. Diesel and steam locomotives and the crack stainless-steel Super Chief had been built as precise copies of the originals, along with bulldozers moving back and forth spreading dirt from a main-line cut, pile drivers, steam shovels, and dump cars. Realistic hillsides were studded with five thousand trees, and elsewhere were mountains, orange groves, deserts, and oil wells. At a master switchboard stood a dispatcher, lights on a diagram before him showing the position of every train and switch. Buttons and levers at spots along the wire netting enclosing the exhibit enabled the demonstrator to stop and start trains and switch them from track to track.

Lohr spent much time after the opening inspecting all exhibits. He had ordered many of the labels and display cards rewritten so as to make them more comprehensible. Some exhibits already had one or more telephones with tape recordings, and Lohr noted closely that visitors spent more time there than at the ones with only printed matter to explain the processes involved. He hoped eventually to persuade exhibitors to install these devices wherever possible, since he realized that by listening to a recorded explanation a visitor felt a greater sense of participation.

As he saw visitors stream into the Museum in larger numbers than previously, he took other measures to insure their return. Aware that few directives annoyed visitors more than to have attendants shout, "Everybody out! Time to close!" Lohr directed that no word be spoken as closing time came, but that, starting at five minutes past the hour, lights be turned off progressively, beginning in the farthest reaches of the Museum. This worked well and visitors began to drift toward the front doors; usually within fifteen minutes they were out, with no feeling that they had been unceremoniously ejected. On rare occasions when visitors showed up past the closing hour they were invited, especially if they were from out of the city, to come in and look around the north court for half an hour. Lohr permitted visitors to smoke and ordered the installation of ash trays and trash cans throughout the institution. Also put into effect was a daily cleanup plan, which called for starting at the front and moving backward through the Museum, and Lohr made it obligatory that all graffiti and assorted wall scribblings be painted over at once.

At this time the Museum's bookstore was started on a modest scale. Checkroom attendants had reported an ever-rising number of requests for pencils and notebooks from visitors. So arrangements were made with one company to furnish notebooks and with another to supply pencils—"Museum of Science and Industry" was imprinted along one side of each pencil, and "Nature supplies the graphite and the wood and industry makes the pencil" along another—and these were placed on sale at the checkroom. When visitors continued to ask checkroom attendants for other items—a guidebook or volumes on subjects dealt with in exhibits—the notion of establishing a book section in the rotunda naturally followed. After conferring with Adolph Kroch, dean of Chicago booksellers, and his son, Carl, about the possibilities of setting up a branch of their bookstore chain in the Museum and determining that this would be uneconomical for both the Krochs and the Museum, a small stall was built and stocked with books and a variety of scientific games. In subsequent years, this was periodically enlarged and diversified so that it became a major attraction in the Museum.

As the new year opened—with an attendance figure for 1940 of 516,848, higher by some forty thousand over 1939's—the hitherto quiescent campaign to increase attendance by school groups was intensified. Earlier, James Rowland Angell, the former Yale University president whom Lohr had engaged as NBC's educational adviser, had paid the Museum a visit to lecture for two days to key staff members on the need for establishing close relations with all schools in and around Chicago. "If you cannot do a good job with the schools," he told them, "you'd better shut your doors, for this is essentially an educational institution." A series of receptions for teachers was instituted, and Lohr conferred with William H. Johnson, superintendent of Chicago schools, who offered to appoint a committee of school administrators to meet with Museum representatives to correlate Museum activities with specific school programs and a schedule of school visits to the Museum. The immediate result was a noticeable increase in this category of visitors, 25,750 from

January to June, compared with 8,323 in the same period the previous year; the long-range effect was a far broader program of organized school tours with monthly study topics and a resultant rise in the ranks of children of school age, who came not only in groups but on weekends and holidays with parents.

To cement further the devoutly wished-for close relationship with visitors of all ages, Lohr ordered the preparation and distribution of leaflets headed, "The Museum Appreciates Your Visit." These asked for answers to questions about residence, age, sex, service in the armed forces, occupation, frequency of visits to the Museum, possible subjects, industries, and products for exhibit, and ultimately, "What suggestions do you have for improving the Museum?" This was more than a token gesture, for through the responses Lohr hoped not only to get clues about exhibits of greatest interest to visitors but to use the data in his presentations to prospective industrial exhibitors. He also gathered other statistics, deriving figures on the extent of out-of-state attendance from a daily check of license plates on automobiles in the parking area. The license-plate survey, Lohr informed the trustees, indicated that on busy summer days nearly every state in the union was represented. And on the first anniversary of the October 26 full opening, Lohr had other gratifying data to report to the trustees. The financial crisis had been alleviated by the economies and $120,000 in museum-tax funds. Expenses were still in excess of income, but the preceding year's deficit had been cut by $170,000. And as for the all-important attendance: the total of 955,813 was almost twice that of the preceding year.

2.

Despite his successes, Lohr was pragmatic enough to realize that with America's involvement in World War II, chances for a strong response to his plan for industrial participation were slim. Most of the companies he had approached or had intended to solicit were involved in war production and not overly inclined to consider immediate participation in Lohr's plans. He continued, however, to extol the long-range institutional benefits of exhibiting in the Museum, and meanwhile he sought attractions that would draw an increase in visitors toward the hoped-for annual mark of one million.

There was, to be sure, a steady flow of military and war-related displays: rubble from London buildings hit in Nazi air attacks, a robot bomb, a British Spitfire, the first public showing of radar devices, a fully rigged model of an American paratrooper, and a variety of home-front activities from courses in how to make nutritious meals despite food rationing and to care for household equipment more efficiently to instruction for American Red Cross workers and motor mechanics. Higgins Industries sought permission to build an exhibit with little more than its famous landing boat as a centerpiece, but Lohr and Massmann persuaded its executives to take a much larger view; the result was a Marine Room, featuring various kinds of Higgins landing craft, supplemented by Museum-owned instruments, gyroscopes, lighthouse lamps, models of ships from the era of the Phoenicians until modern days, and murals showing how an amphibious fleet was planned and constructed. In a two-storied hall the Navy constructed the bridge of a destroyer complete with charthouse, steering gear, and range finder, and with depth charges, mine sweepers' paravanes, and torpedo tubes. To this strikingly effective exhibit came not only civilians by the many thousands but midshipmen from Abbott Hall on Northwestern University's Chicago campus, just as trainees from the Navy's aviation machinists' school at Navy Pier and Army Signal Corps cadets at the University of Chicago came to study other exhibits in their fields. Flags of the anti-Axis nations were arranged in a panoply inside the entrance to the north court and remained for the war's duration.

One of the few new industrial exhibits opened toward the end of 1941 was that of the Carborundum Company of Niagara Falls, New York. It traced the history of the manufacture of modern abrasives from the laboratory of Dr. Edward Goodrich Acheson in Monongahela City, Pennsylvania, where he created the first man-made abrasive, silicon carbide, to which he affixed the name Carborundum. Near a worktable was a revolving mound of vari-colored crystals set on a circular block of black marble. A series of dioramas portrayed the types of electric furnaces that had long since supplanted Dr. Acheson's iron pots and the manifold crushing and grading operations involved in production of modern abrasive products. Although the exhibit lacked the kind of action and movement sought, Lohr was pleased to have it and doubly pleased with the comment of an editorialist in *Industrial Arts and Vocational Education:* "The Carborundum Co. is to be commended for this fine piece of educational work. The value of industrial museums is only slowly being understood, and it is to be hoped that other nationally known producers of the various articles now in common use will follow this latest example and offer the public a similar opportunity to learn about other interesting phases of our complex industrial civilization. The interest value of such industrial museum exhibits is great, but the educational value to young and old alike is very much greater."

Later, as the Museum's financial structure continued to grow stronger, several projects financed by a $125,000 grant from the Rosenwald Family Association were undertaken, principally one depicting the principles of magnetism and another that used five microprojectors secured from the Buhl Planetarium, in Pittsburgh, for the projection of live microorganisms on a large screen.

Interestingly, and somewhat ironically, two of the Museum's projects that originated in this period and maintained their popularity year after year well into the present had very little to do either with science or industry. Yet they were in accord with Lohr's concept that a certain percentage of permanent attractions fit logically into the over-all format purely as "entertainment features" that could lure a certain percentage of visitors who would then also turn to exhibits of more vital importance.

The first of these stemmed from Lohr's desire to boost December attendance, traditionally lower than in any other month, and to pay recognition to ethnic groups in Chicago allied with the war effort. Martha McGrew suggested that by working with the various local consuls, each day in the two weeks preceding Christmas could be devoted to a specific group with the huge Christmas tree in the rotunda decorated in the tradition of the country represented and with native dishes featured on the dining-room menu.

On December 11, 1942, Greek Day initiated the project. Flags of twenty-nine nations were unfurled beneath the balcony of the north court, and on successive days the tree was trimmed and then untrimmed and retrimmed for such other countries as Mexico, Czechoslovakia, Holland, Belgium, Soviet Russia, Yugoslavia, Poland, the British Empire, China, a variety of South American countries, and the United States. Special efforts were made to publicize the event by sending stories to foreign-language newspapers and personal letters to principals of all schools in the Chicago area and by placing thirty thousand circulars in forty different places throughout the city, in addition to arranging for considerable coverage by the metropolitan and neighborhood newspapers and radio stations.

Thus, "Christmas Around the World" was launched, presumably to continue forever. Its popularity—and publicity—has never slackened. In 1943 a Dutch group from Holland, Michigan, needed a large white horse for its Saint Nicholas to ride in its pageant, "Sinter Klaas Day." Miss McGrew learned that a steed could be rented for the day for $150, a sum her budget could not allow. So she wrote a letter to the *Tribune*, explaining her plight and suggesting that the newspaper, with its vast influence and resources could surely come to her aid. On the day the newspaper printed her letter, some two hundred offers were received, and she gratefully accepted a handsome horse from Keith Line, operator of the Midway Stables, a mile from the Museum.

In subsequent years, in addition to an eighteen-foot tree decorated in typically American style with colored electric lights, bright baubles, tinsel, and simulated snow, trees of other nations have been arranged in a circle around it. Each is, of course, decked in native style, starting on Thanksgiving Day, when tree trimmers, most of them in folk attire of their land of origin, arrive to go to work. Every year, the hall has become ablaze with light and color and decorations—Dutch tulips and wooden show ornaments, Mexican piñatas, crèches from Ireland and Italy, Czech dolls, garlands of Swedish and Norwegian miniature flags, Lithuanian straw in intricate geometric designs, and, in the postwar years, German gingerbread angels, shepherds, and animals, and Japanese lanterns and rice wafers with fortunes enclosed—and in the dining room visitors sampled veal soup from Slovenia or beef birds from Lithuania or beet soup from Poland. And the crowds, of course, have multiplied. In the second year of the event, instead of the usual December count of thirty thousand, no fewer than 130,000 came to the Museum, a pace that has not only prevailed but heightened annually.

The other of these perennially popular attractions grew out of the problem of what to do with antiques and historical items stacked in warehouses or in the Museum's storeroom and the donation of several antique automobiles by D. Cameron Peck, a Bowman Dairy Company executive and neighbor of Lohr's. Peck had interested Lohr in the car-collecting hobby, and originally Lohr intended to display

Peck's vehicles in a section to be called "Street of Old Autos." But this basic concept soon developed into what came to be "Yesterday's Main Street," a block-long reproduction of an early-twentieth-century Chicago thoroughfare, with store-front and show-window exhibits by well-known and long-established local firms, an old-fashioned nickelodeon with such features as *The Great Train Robbery*, *Border Laws*, and *Cowboys and Indians*, and a lineup of antique automobiles including some of Lohr's and an electric-powered one that had been owned by the famous University of Chicago football coach Amos Alonzo Stagg. These cars constituted one of three separate exhibits of vintage automobiles in the Museum, ranging from an 1893 Bernardi with side steering wheel and an 1896 Benz to a 1909 Sears Roebuck buggy roadster, a 1912 Stanley Steamer capable of speeds up to 160 miles an hour, and a 1913 White National with running boards commodious enough to accommodate eight people. To those who wondered what connection "Yesterday's Main Street" had with the general purpose of the Museum, Lohr had a ready reply. "There is the scientific story of the development of the automobile," he wrote in the invitation to the preview on July 12, 1943, "but there is another story which refreshes more memories. It's the human side of the automobile and the people who used them and cared for them. It's the story of linen dusters and clincher tires, of carbide lamps and hay wire, of side curtains and bent wish bones." And it was a story that obviously held strong interest for those who came then and later, for "Yesterday's Main Street" has continued as a Museum favorite.

3.

Because the Museum was classified as a non-essential industry instead of an educational institution, many of the younger staff members became eligible for military service. As those who were drafted and others with reserve commissions departed, it was difficult to find adequate replacements. For a time, younger visitors with scientific interests or training were recruited to serve as demonstrators with red-white-and-blue badges and a ranking of "Guide Buddy." With many key staff members, especially from the technical and engineering sections, gone, Lohr was hard-pressed to secure replacements and multiplied the duties of the remaining staff members so that none of the Museum's activities might be neglected.

In this period, too, he was able to obtain the part-time services of Harvey B. Lemon, a University of Chicago physicist, as curator of physical sciences. Lemon's association not only would prove vastly beneficial—he soon was named scientific director and gave sage counsel on many scientific exhibits other than those in his field of specialization—but served to develop more closely the ties that already prevailed with the university's chemistry department. By now Arthur Holly Compton was a trustee, and with Professor Lemon as a staff member, Lohr lost little time in expanding the affiliation. He held a number of meetings with the university's president, Robert Maynard Hutchins, and effected an arrangement in which, by the end of 1944, twenty-three members of the faculty were working on a number of cooperative plans, including a study by Professor Louis L. Thurstone, the internationally famed psychologist, and his associates to determine the exhibits' educational value. In addition, Hutchins extended Lemon's leave for as long as the Museum deemed necessary and authorized other professors as needed to participate in an effort to raise the general level of exhibits in the physical and biological sciences and a long-range study of how to design and use exhibits with other educational techniques—"a fertile field," as Lohr described it to his trustees, "for the exploration of the psychology of Museum showmanship." This relationship

Long one of the Museum's most alluring attractions in the Swift
& Company's "Food for Life" exhibit is this poultry incubator,
where visitors can watch baby chicks emerging from their shells.

At the General Motors "Motorama" exhibit, a youngster manipulates a hand braking device.

Daniel M. MacMaster explains one of the many installations in the Standard Oil (Ind.) Foundation's spectacular exhibit tracing the exploration for and uses of petroleum.

The drawing room of Colleen Moore's famous Fairy Castle, whose popularity since its installation, in 1949, has grown steadily.

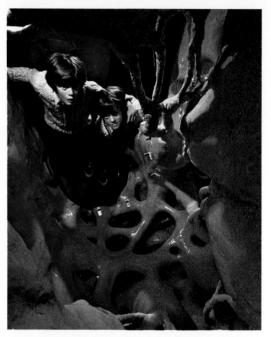

"The largest heart in the world" is a 14-foot, precisely structured model through which visitors can walk and examine all parts. It is a prime feature of the Chicago Heart Association's exhibit.

"Harvester Farm," the International Harvester Company's exhibit, is a life-size reproduction of a fully mechanized midwestern farm, complete with rolling fields, equipment, and barns.

Youngsters are fascinated by the light bulbs that are used to demonstrate the multiplication table in IBM's "Mathematica" exhibit.

A portion of the Museum's East Court, showing a variety of airplanes hanging from the ceiling and part of the Santa Fe Railway's 3,000-square-foot model of its transcontinental system.

In the Bell Telephone System's "Hall of Communications," a favorite attraction is the telephone on which this caller can hear precisely how her voice sounds in transmission.

Below, latest photographic techniques—ranging from use of ultrapowerful lenses to see microworlds of color, pattern, and texture, to lensless cameras with laser beams—are in the Eastman Kodak Company's striking "This is Photography" exhibit.

Children gather at the "Focus on Environment" sector of "Showcase for Steel," one of the Museum's most extensive exhibits, sponsored by the country's foremost steelmaking companies.

A perennial favorite is "Yesterday's Main Street," a reproduction of an American street of the early part of the century, featuring gas street lights, antique automobiles, and a nickelodeon.

Victor J. Danilov, named the Museum's director in 1972, visits with students in the "Mathematica" exhibit.

would have many results beneficial to both Museum and university and in addition served as a goad to enlist support, as was done in subsequent years, of faculties and officials of other universities.

4.

As the war neared its end, prospects for the future were favorable. Even early in 1944 renewed interest was shown by major firms, with visits to the Museum by delegations from the General Motors Corporation, Ansco Company, and Sears Roebuck and Co., and Lohr was on the verge of closing a contract with International Harvester Company. The Museum's financial condition had grown progressively better; 1943 was the last year to show an operating deficit, the figure of $15,800 representing a reduction of $329,307 from the deficit of 1940. Fortunately Sears Roebuck and Co. stock had risen considerably in value, with a corresponding boost in dividends, and the board had ventured into diversification of its holdings in 1945, selling five thousand shares worth over $625,000 to buy blue-chip securities in eleven companies ranging from General Motors and American Telephone and Telegraph to Eastman Kodak and Dow Chemical. And attendance had, in 1942, gone over the hoped-for one million. In that year, 1,104,605 people had come to the Museum, a mark, Lohr was quick to note to the board, that was exceeded only by New York's Museum of Natural History. Although the 1943 attendance dropped to 901,292, in 1944 it was 1,021,048, never again to go lower.

The crisis Lohr had inherited in the summer of 1940 had been effectively weathered, the serious problems confronted and conquered, the Museum's philosophy articulately and firmly established. There was no way to go but forward, and in that direction and toward new goals Lohr now pointed his ambitions and his hopes.

CHAPTER X

FARMS, BABIES, AND AUTOS

In the two years after the end of World War II, three major exhibits were created that would not only, in the short run, validate Lohr's basic theories of what purposes the Museum could best serve, but would endure, with revisions and improvements wherever necessary, as important and mutually beneficial attractions persistently popular with the public.

The campaign to gain the first of these had begun in 1942, with letters and statistics to the potential sponsor, the International Harvester Company, one of the largest makers of farm implements and machinery in the world. Paul Massmann took the initiative in proposing erection of an exhibit to emphasize the company's role in war production. He stressed to company officials the growing public acceptance of the Museum as indicated by increases in yearly attendance and in average length of visits (fifty-five minutes in 1940, 192 minutes in 1942). Discussions continued and reached a point where a letter of agreement was drawn, but at the end of 1944 emphasis had switched, as Massmann wrote to the firm's public-relations chief, Dale Cox, to an exhibit depicting the mechanization of agriculture, because "the company represents such great achievements in this field." More meetings and conferences followed, with the result that by February 1945 basic themes ("Agriculture is a fundamental of the American way of life" and "The agriculturist is a business man with specialized knowledge") were established, and Raymond Loewy was selected by company officials as chief designer. What with shortages of essential building materials and other problems, it was not until July 3, 1946, that the exhibit was ready for public inspection.

The earlier ideas had been discarded by Loewy and the Harvester people in favor of a "Harvester Farm" spread over the whole of the west court and complete in every detail, down to such sound effects as roosters crowing, hens clucking, cows mooing, and woodpeckers tapping tattoos. A colonial-style farmhouse, so designed after thousands of farm families all over the country had been asked in a formal survey about their preferences on style and content, contained a sleek kitchen with a host of appliances, cabinets, an electric range, and a spacious freezer, a small office for the farmer in which to work on his records, a privet-hedged rear porch from which could be viewed synthetic fields of corn, wheat, alfalfa, and other crops, each with its appropriate International Harvester machine for planting, cultivating, or harvesting. In the driveway stood the familiar International Harvester pickup truck loaded with milk cans, and across the driveway from the farmhouse a brooder house filled with baby chicks. Elsewhere in the area were a silo, machines capable of such tasks as baling six tons of hay in an hour and cultivating two rows of corn in a single movement, a forge, a workshop, and a machine shed containing such other company products as a grain drill, a manure spreader, a corn planter, and a self-propelled harvester-thresher, latest in the long line of grain-harvesting devices since Cyrus McCormick's 1831 reaper. A commodious barn contained a sheep pen and milking stall in which stood five pure-bred cows mounted by a skilled taxidermist, Julius Friesser of the Chicago Natural History Museum. One of them, a Holstein, was fully animated so that her eyes, mouth, and tail moved and she could be milked with a modern milking machine. A search had been conducted all over the country for this Holstein and sterling representatives of such other especially productive breeds of American dairy cattle as Jersey, Guernsey, Brown Swiss, and Ayrshire. The perfect specimens had then been turned over to Friesser, who, after supervising their slaughter, spent eight months in building five frames of wire, burlap, and adhesive before mounting the carcasses. Past a corncrib and hog lot was a lounge adjoining a small theater, where a movie every hour showed the latest agricultural methods and machines. Cox devised a vast publicity campaign, sending stories to four thousand daily and weekly newspapers, running three-quarter-page advertisements in the Chicago papers, arranging for frequent radio broadcasts, and preparing a descriptive pamphlet, one hundred thousand copies of which were run off in the initial printing.

The exhibit was an instant success, with 80 to 90 per cent of all visitors pausing to spend time there. All personnel looked and listened for the first week and prepared detailed memos for Lohr not only about crowd reactions but on myriad matters relating to the model farm. In the farm house, installation of built-in smoking stands was recommended, because on the very first day, the ash trays were stolen and visitors were strewing ashes on the floor. The glass encasing the milk stalls needed to be raised and extended to keep people from twisting off the cows' tails. Larger ventilating fans were installed in the farmhouse's living room and kitchen, and a lock was put on the farm mailbox, because half a dozen letters ready for the post office had been deposited in it along with a bundle of religious tracts.

International Harvester Company officials were obviously pleased with what had been wrought, for in 1956 they authorized expenditures for major alterations to form a new, nineteen thousand-square-foot "Farm and City" exhibit, which, in the words of the company's chairman, John L. McCaffrey, showed "the interrelationship between farm and city families and the interdependence of these two major groups in our civilization today." Dominating the reshaped and enlarged exhibit was a ten-foot figure of a man on a revolving pedestal. One side of him was a man of a century ago, indicating—and a lighted sign so stated—that it then took the work of a single farmer to feed five people; the other was of a modern farmer, whose sign informed viewers that he, using modern farm machinery, could feed twenty persons. New items on the farm reflected new living habits, such as an all-gas kitchen installed by the Peoples Gas Light and Coke Company, a flagstone patio with a barbecue grill, and a television set. An expanded network of push buttons set off the various harvesting and planting machines. New stalls were built in the barn for use on special occasions such as the Easter holiday season, when the inevitable attraction was a pair of rabbits and their multitudinous offspring.

As it maintained its attraction as a major exhibit, the Harvester Farm served to support Lohr's aim to remind the public of the integration of science and industry to help form a strong national economy. To some, this may have seemed too simplistic and to minimize social implications, but Lohr could not agree. The Museum's primary task, he persistently emphasized, was to tell a story and let viewers make conclusions, and not engage in complexities that could engender intense controversy. In the case of the Harvester Farm, Lohr felt the basic mission was well accomplished and that it demonstrated, as the firm's president, Frank W. Jenks, noted in a ceremony marking the exhibit's fifteenth year at the Museum, "how farming and industry are the two great pillars of our economic and social life and how each serves the other."

2.

Long before advocates of sex education for school children broadened and intensified their efforts, the Museum of Science and Industry was well in the forefront of this movement with an exhibit that, in Lohr's words, "not only tells a story for both children and adults in a dignified, appealing and highly instructive manner but may represent a new departure in displays of this kind, concerned with the important subject of health, a story which needs imagination and vigor in telling, and for which the public is waiting."

Considered daring and, to some, highly controversial, this exhibit, aptly called "Miracle of Growth," graphically showed human development from embryonic life through adolescence, from conception to maturity. Prepared in cooperation with the medical staff of the University of Illinois, the exhibit's most striking element was a life-size, transparent figure of a pregnant woman in whose womb of soft plastic lay a fetus at the end of its period of intrauterine life just before the onset of labor and the dramatic process of birth. Then, in a series of panels were depicted, through drawings and plaster figures, the process of conception, complete with male and female genitalia and magnified ovum and sperm, and the life of the fetus at various points in a nine-month pregnancy, actual birth through three main stages with life-size models, diagrams of a breech birth, a delivery of mature twins, and a Caesarean birth, care of the newly born infant, and various aspects of growth and development from preschool years through adolescence. A final push-button panel offered replies to questions most frequently asked about heredity. Extending almost the length of the display was a mural illustrating the seven ages of man—from "the infant, / Mewling and puking in the nurse's arms" to "second childishness and mere oblivion" —described by William Shakespeare in *As You Like It*.

During the two years the exhibit was in preparation, questions arose about whether, because of the subject matter and possible adverse reaction, the exhibit should be open one day for females and another for males or if children under seven should be denied admission. The decision was especially sound: No limitations of any sort, since such action would perpetuate the very ills the exhibit was designed to overcome and would stimulate abnormal curiosity about a natural process that needed to be accepted in a matter-of-fact way. Once opened to the public, on August 6, 1947, "Miracle of Growth" then and later aroused immense interest as one of the Museum's most discussed and avidly attended exhibits, and though viewed by well over fifteen million men, women, and children, not a single letter or voiced complaint has been received by Museum officials against it.

This is not to say that many visitors are not startled when they encounter the plastic pregnant lady for the first time. Demonstrators have reported on statements and conversations of visitors of all ages, and over the years these constitute a virtual thesaurus of comment, ranging from amazing ignorance to self-conscious embarrassment to perceptive praise. In the lore surrounding the remarkable display are recalled the visitors who asked, "Where is the exhibit that tells you—well, tells you things?" or "Where's that naked, pregnant woman I read in the paper about?" or "Where is the machine that tells you how your child is going to look?" And the little boy who asked, "Are they all upside down?" and at his mother's affirmative reply, snapped, "Well, I wasn't"; and the ten-year-old girl who stared and said, "No wonder her stomach sticks out!" and one young woman saying to another, "When we have babies, we will have to come here to see how they are"; and the member of a group of young girls who left her companions at the first panel, dashed down the line, and returned to announce, "It's a boy!"

Physicians and other medical men always have been high in their praise of "Miracle of Growth." Many have sent patients, woefully uninformed about such matters, to the Museum to study the exhibit, and since the beginning many hundreds of letters have been received from doctors praising it. Dr. Arnold Gesell, director of Yale University's Clinic of Child Development, was the main speaker at a preview at the time of the exhibit's debut, and then and later, in a handsomely produced and designed book published for the Museum by the University of Illinois Press, eloquently spoke of the exhibit's importance and meaning: "The task of science is to give us knowledge which will help us to understand ourselves and the world in which we live. There are many things to understand. At one extreme is the atom; at another extreme is the child. In the 'Miracle of Growth' these two extremes meet. . . . By portraying the growth of the child in a dramatic manner, the Museum pays its respects to the dignity of the individual. We are indebted to science and to the imaginative persons of good will who have made this unique visual presentation possible." Since "Miracle of Growth" opened, another exhibit, prepared by Dr. J. M. Essenberg of Loyola University's Stritch School of Medicine shows forty stages of development from fertilization of the ovum to the full term of actual embryos and fetuses. Together the two supply scientifically correct information vividly and authentically to all who seek other than curbstone legends and back-yard myths about human reproduction.

3.

One of the very first companies Lohr had hoped to secure as a prime exhibitor in the months after becoming the Museum's president in 1940 was the vast General Motors Corporation. Lohr had been impressed by the company's exhibits at A Century of Progress and by its "Futurama" at the 1939 New York World's Fair, a spectacle that drew some twenty-three million people to look at concepts of forthcoming innovations in superhighway development, and he yearned to secure this giant among auto makers. Approaches had been made, but wartime building restrictions and shortages of essential materials had caused delays. From time to time, however, officials of the firm paid visits to the Museum, and Lohr maintained steady contacts. By October 1944 he could happily report to his trustees that on a recent visit to the General Motors plant in Detroit, he had been assured that a substantial sum had been appropriated for an exhibit for which plans had been formulated and on which, when the war ended and restrictions were lifted, work would start.

Interest in such an exhibit was heightened several months later, when announcement was made of the celebration, under auspices of the Museum, of the fiftieth anniversary of the founding of the automotive industry. To major automobile makers, associations, and scientific groups allied to the industry were mailed five thousand announcements telling of a month-long series of activities in November ranging from special displays of antique automobiles to daily parades of clothing fashions of the preceding half century and culminating in a re-enactment of a widely heralded race on Thanksgiving Day 1895 of what were called "motorcycles." For that event, J. Frank Duryea, promised to be on hand. He had been winner of the original race in the "Buggynaut," built by his brother, Charles, the pioneer among American auto builders and the first ever to use pneumatic rubber tires. The 1895, race, which Hermann H. Kohlsaat, dynamic publisher of the Chicago *Times-Herald* had been inspired to sponsor upon reading in *L'Illustration* of the Paris-to-Rome contest earlier that year, had done much to arouse public interest in the new-fangled invention. Duryea had outlasted three other automatic gasoline carriages and two electric cars over a fifty-four-mile route in seven hours fifty-three minutes to win the two thousand dollar prize. Because of blizzardlike weather, only his car and another had finished. The other car had been piloted by one of the umpires, Charles B. King, after the driver lost consciousness because of the extreme cold. Now Duryea and King, both in their late seventies, returned to ride in ancient cars and join in the re-enactment. Among the early vehicles were an 1896 Baker Electric, a 1905 Mier, a 1907 Schacht, a 1909 Cadillac, and a 1909 Holsman-Stanhope. The event was less a race than a parade, with the cars leisurely traveling north on Lake Shore Drive, their drivers—including Lohr—tooting horns and waving hands at passing motorists. The event was well covered in the local newspapers and by a Fox Movietone newsreel cameraman, Fred "Red" Felbinger, who recorded it on film for exhibition in thousands of movie theaters—and with a special print made for the General Motors officials involved in carrying through plans for the exhibit.

Because of its scope—eventually it covered over eleven thousand square feet—the General Motors exhibit, called "Motorama," was nearly two years in the making. Lohr urged inclusion of attractions that would heighten visitor participation—a manually operated transmission or brake or devices to show foot-pounds of work done by a modern starter—and Massmann also sought ideas and suggestions from steel, oil, and rubber companies traditionally allied with the automotive industry. As the time for the scheduled opening approached, meticulous attention was paid to myriad details, from the number and placement of sand jars to protect carpeting from dropped cigar and cigarette ashes to securing needed additional electrical power by asking officials of the Argonne National Laboratory, the vast atomic-energy complex then a-building southwest of the city, to close their office in the Museum an hour earlier than usual.

"Motorama" opened on November 14, 1947. In the Theme Room a brightly colored mural depicting the evolution of land, sea, and air transportation flanked a display of eleven types of wheels from prehistoric log types and Babylonian chariot disks through those used on Conestoga wagons and Napoleonic carriages to the most recent American vehicles. A one-cylinder Oldsmobile, the Scout, the first gasoline-engine, mass-produced auto, famed for a forty-four-day trip from New York to Portland, Oregon, in 1905, revolved on a turntable, and nearby were panels displaying sources of power (winds, water, heat from fuels and sun, atomic energy, and muscular energy) and primary machines (screw, lever, pulley, wedge, wheel and axle, and inclined plane) and displays showing elements of combustion and internal combustion. A doorway of the Theme Room led directly to the popular "Yesterday's Main Street," with its lineup of antique autos. The adjoining Hall of Development was replete with all manner of devices essential to the manufacture and operation of automobiles, a 1912 Buick engine complete with hand crank, a model of Charles F. Kettering's famous self-starter, which he had developed in a barn in Dayton, Ohio, in 1911, models of the first V-8 engines, and cars that originated use of curved glass. Visitors could operate many devices here and in the Hall of Engineering, where sliding gears illustrated the basic principle of power or of power steering; they could light up dioramas in other sections portraying the workings of diesel engines, early and modern production methods, and such company products as console radios, helicopters, electric stoves, refrigerators, and freezers. "Today's Street" was a corridor with window displays of automobile appliances and accessories and travel scenes with an assortment of fourteen free booklets bearing such titles as *Power Goes to Work, Transporta-*

tion Progress, The Automobile User's Guide, and *We Drivers.*

As ever, incisive reports were prepared both for Museum officials and General Motors representatives on needed improvements, changes, and alterations, any criticism softened by an espousal of basic tenets: "As we are a Museum of science and industry, the public expects meticulous accuracy in all exhibits. Poetic and artistic license which would be acceptable elsewhere, as at trade shows, has the effect here of creating distrust and skepticism in the minds of the visitors. They had learned to expect here not only that the laws of nature are immutable, but that their portrayal be without flaw. Many of our visitors are quick to pick up the slighest technical inaccuracy. It is because of this that seemingly trivial things assume considerable importance." Among the "seemingly trivial things" noted in memos to Lohr from staff members after the opening were:

There should be a wood plug over the axle of the Babylonian chariot wheel.

The lettering "1900–1904 Olds Runabout" should be painted off the front and this information put on a small sign near enough to the car to identify it.

A new handle should be installed on the Buick crank; present one is dangerous. Motor should be oiled. Grease cups and other parts must be fastened down.

Rug should be provided in front of Brake Exhibit, since pressure of feet in one place will quickly wear a hole in the carpet.

Wall in east court adjacent to exit should be painted.

Oldsmobile Scout is touched by almost everyone. Many try to see how fast they can revolve the platform by hand and whether it can be stalled.

Even if it does no damage, the psychology is if you
get away with it there to try it all over the Museum.

Modern car should have gas tank and hood
locked.

By the end of the exhibit's first month, 121,242 persons
had visited "Motorama." Most of the comments made to
or overheard by demonstrators were favorable. Representatives of other auto manufacturers paid respectful visits and
offered compliments, although some felt the exhibit was too
technical in spots for the average visitor and others that
an attempt had been made to tell too much in the space
available for the visitor to absorb in the time available.
General Motors executives were highly pleased. W. G.
Lewellen, a vice-president, wrote to Lohr, "We feel very
proud of the exhibit and the opportunity we have through
it to make a contribution to a greater knowledge of the
automobile business—what it has done, is doing and hopes
to do to make available more and better things for more
people." Lohr replied in kind: "From all points of view
this is the finest industrial exhibition in existence. The contribution it is making day after day is tremendous."

The relationship has persisted well into the present. In
1958, an almost entirely new "Motorama" replaced the first
exhibit, and two years later an even more modernized,
fifty-six-unit version was installed, retaining the most pertinent elements of the older ones and placing greater emphasis on research and developments for the future. Visitors
can manipulate analog and digital computers, learn the
binary number system, and play complex mathematical
games, all as a means of illustrating modernized methods
used in auto production. From General Motors Research
Laboratories came a mechanical heart, complete with a
plasma and vaccine sterilizer that used neither heat nor
chemicals, and an "automatic highway" with innumerable
safety devices. In a new Hall of Tomorrow are panoramic

displays showing progress in safety measures over the decades and possible uses of solar energy and atomic engines. Invariably intent on keeping its exhibit popular (more than thirty-five million visitors since 1947) and contemporary, the company most recently added devices whose purpose is to cut down on use of substances that cause pollutants to enter the atmosphere.

4.

The opening of these three important and long-enduring exhibits in a single year gave considerable justification to Lohr's year-end report that "1947 has been the year of greatest public service in the institution's history." Moreover, its financial stability had been enhanced, its reputation as a foremost tourist attraction strengthened, and its attendance—always so vital to its fate—continued to climb, to a new record of 1,360,445.

CHAPTER XI

THE NATION TAKES NOTICE

Conditions at the Museum were now so roseate that Lohr readily agreed to organize and run a new fair to commemorate the one hundredth anniversary of the first run, in 1848, of Mayor William B. Ogden's tiny Pioneer locomotive; on that historic trip, the Pioneer had hauled a flatcar packed with city officials on a five-mile trip north from Chicago. As president of the Chicago Railroad Fair, which had first been proposed by the *Tribune*, Lohr chose Daniel MacMaster to be general manager. Lohr had come to rely on MacMaster not only to assume increasing supervision of the Museum but also to appear before civic groups and varied organizations to make speeches, a task Lohr invariably carried out with little relish, but which MacMaster, articulate and knowledgeable, performed to good effect.

The general plan involved enlistment of support from the country's railroads large and small and from their principal equipment suppliers—notably builders of locomotives and cars—for a summer-season fair that would combine recreation and instruction in exhibits designed to lure visitors from many states. The site selected was a fifty-acre strip on the lakefront where once had stood the "Belgian Village" and the lively "Streets of Paris" of A Century of Progress. "Chicago Railroad Fair will be designed to bring home to

hundreds of thousands of Americans," read the official pro-
spectus, "the contributions the railroads of the nation have
made in the settlement of the country, in the development
of its economy, in the winning of its wars, and in the
constant elevation of its standard of living. Chicago Railroad
Fair also will be employed to indicate how the railroads of
the nation will contribute greatly to the future progress of
the country and finally to illustrate the railroads' continuing
effort to assure their millions of patrons constantly higher
standards of service, convenience, comfort and safety."

The mounting challenges of travel by air and the eventual
massive woes of the railroad industry were years away as
preparations were made for the opening on July 20, 1948.
From the start, the fair was a hit. Lohr insisted that prices
be kept as low as possible. Consequently, for less than a
dollar a visitor could buy a ticket, attend "Wheels A-Rolling," a pageant presented four times a day to dramatize
the history of the railroads as it related to the growth of
the nation, and ride the length of the fair grounds on the
Deadwood Central, a narrow-gauge train of the kind used
in the mountains of the Old West. "Wheels A-Rolling" was
conceived by Helen Tieken Geraghty, an experienced theat-
rical producer and former actress, and Edward Hungerford;
it was performed against the backdrop of Lake Michigan
by 220 actors on a stage broad and large enough to tell the
story from the crude travois of Indians and such famed
early trains as the Best Friend of Charleston of 1830 and the
William Mason of 1856 to the newest diesel-powered luxury
streamliners. Although the *Tribune* had originated the idea,
one of the brightest tributes came from Robert Pollak, drama
critic of the rival *Sun-Times:* "As every schoolboy knows,
any old pageant can be pretty dull business, but the people
concerned in this dramatic history of America on wheels
have done a yeoman job and given their huge show plenty
of movement and sweep and a judicious mixture of senti-
ment and humor. . . . 'Wheels A-Rolling' is a painless lesson

in history, a shrewd sample of the ancient art of pageantry and a thumping good piece of entertainment."

Elsewhere the attractions included the Santa Fe Railway's Indian village, whose 125 inhabitants representing six tribes engaged in the making of blankets, dolls, moccasins, and pottery, the weaving of baskets and belts, and silversmithing; a replica of the original Pioneer; a complete pine forest transplanted from the northwest; such regional representations as an orange grove, a dude ranch, the geyser Old Faithful in Yellowstone National Park, and scores of famed trains.

By the fair's end, early in October, well over 2,500,000 persons had come through the gates. In typical fashion, Lohr offered significant statistics to reporters: More than half had seen the pageant; 950,000 had ridden on the Deadwood Central; 13,958 meals had been served in the Rock Island's dining car, and other restaurants on the grounds had served one million meals; 28 per cent of the paid admissions were by persons who had seen the fair before and were returning for another look; half of the total attendance was from outside Illinois; the working staff of five hundred spent an average of fifteen hours a day at their labors. As for finances, gross revenues from the seventy-six-day exposition totaled $1,225,000, a fraction of the total value of exhibits. But the purpose of the fair had never been to create profit, and the thirty-eight participating railroads considered their contributions—the larger ones invested seventy-five thousand dollars each—money well spent in a good-will project designed to give visitors enjoyment and show them entertainingly the part that railroads had played in the country's economy and growth.

2.

Lohr's supervision of the Chicago Railroad Fair and MacMaster's management had been so astute and efficient that both found sufficient time to devote to Museum activities. With the new year, Lohr, as ever, was eager for reports on annual attendance figures and pleased to learn that a new record, of 1,410,445, had been set in 1948, although for this fifteenth anniversary year he had hoped to reach and even top 1,500,000.

In 1949 he yearned to attain new records, and there were new exhibits to help him do so: the "Story of Aluminum," sponsored by the Aluminum Company of America; the Bakelite Corporation's Hall of Plastics; the Illinois Division of the American Cancer Society's striking series of pictures dealing with the symptoms, spread, and treatment of the disease; a United States Naval Ordnance Bureau display of naval firepower; "Yesterday's Firefighters," a collection of historic fire-fighting equipment sponsored by the local insurance firm of Marsh and McLennan; a "Wheels A-Rolling" room containing many of the ancient vehicles of the 1948 fair's pageant. Additional national publicity was secured. An essay contest in the Boston *Post* offered as first prize a trip to what the newspaper described as "The most famous Museum in the United States today." Ben Hibbs, editor of *The Saturday Evening Post*, was persuaded by Norbert Hildebrand, the Museum's publicity director since 1947, to assign a writer, Harland Manchester, to spend a week; the result was a lushly illustrated article titled "Museums Don't Have to be Stuffy," in which Manchester recorded the historical background, the crucial role played by Julius Rosenwald, Lohr's reversal of the Museum's fortunes in 1940, and his many actions to transform it into a crowd-attracting, crowd-pleasing, yet educational and instructive, institution. Manchester estimated the value of industrial exhibits at five million dollars, expressed delight with the idea of visitor participation ("Everywhere there is light, color and movement, and you are a part of it. You push buttons and turn cranks, and things happen, and the first thing you know you have learned something"), described in vivid detail such favorite attractions among the two hundred as the coal mine, the "Harvester Farm," "Yesterday's Main Street," and "Miracle of Growth," and spoke approvingly of the philosophy of industrial participation: "From the start, Major Lohr has been careful to forestall any fears by educators that the Museum would become unduly commercialized. . . . Its prestige warns would-be exhibitors that this is not a trade show. This industrial-participation plan is so unusual that its program manager, Paul Massmann, once an ace high-pressure salesman for fairs and exhibitions, now calls himself a 'low-pressure' salesman."

Manchester took special note of the enthusiasm expressed by educators—George D. Stoddard, president of the University of Illinois, President Henry T. Heald of the Illinois Institute of Technology, Herold C. Hunt, general superintendent of Chicago's schools, Dean Walter C. Bartky of the University of Chicago's physical sciences division—for the Museum's method of informally educating masses of school children. Earlier efforts to systematize and increase visits by school groups had been given great impetus in 1946 when Harry Orrin Gillet, recently retired as principal of the University of Chicago's laboratory school, joined the staff to help train demonstrators and devise programs for school tours. Gillet worked assiduously at both assignments together with Harvey Lemon and Martha McGrew. They worked out specific programs in which booklets were sent each September to public, parochial, and private elementary and high schools in the Chicago area, denoting tour topics for each month of the coming year ("Forests and Forest Products," "The Story of the Newspaper," "Some Topics in General Science," "Iron, Oil and Coal," "Physiology and Health," and others dealing with transportation, microscopic living animals, magnetism, electricity, telephones, radio, sound, and light). In addition, expanded announcements were sent every month, typical of which was one on "Graphic Arts and History of Telling Time":

"Although we are sometimes embarrassed by the number of classes being brought to the Museum, we continue to extend a cordial invitation. We are equipped to provide a unique kind of visual education, the seeing of actual things in operation. In some fields this contributes better even than motion pictures to realization and understanding.

"The exhibit of graphic arts is an especially good example of effective presentation. We are making a feature of it in the December school tour. The students will see how type is set by hand and how the compositor observes the rules of English usage taught in schools and gives consideration to the appearance of the page. Then they will see a proof pulled and corrections made. Finally they will observe the operation of the press. Instead of setting the type by hand, the demonstrator may use the linotype machine.

"The exhibit includes a remarkable representation of a monk in his cell copying and illuminating a manuscript. Something of the history of printing appears in the models of old presses. But it is the modern in the graphic arts that occupies the greater space. The procedures from the taking of the photograph or the making of a drawing to the picture in the newspaper or magazine are adequately shown. The printing of colored pictures by using in succession inks of primary colors always proves instructive to students.

"The demonstrator will, if requested, tell about the making of a newspaper, from the writing of the news 'story' to the operations of the huge rotary press. This will be of special benefit to classes interested in the school newspaper.

"A second feature of the school tour for December is the exhibit of the history of telling time through the ages. It is a long story, this history, but the Elgin Watch Company tells it briefly and adequately in a series of models of many old devices followed by scores of watches from the earliest to the very accurate watch movements of today. The demonstrator will take the class from section to section and finally to the large model of the instrument by the use of which time can be told by the stars."

In groups usually averaging fifty but sometimes running as high as one hundred, students and teachers came prepared to spend at least three hours on a specific tour. Initially, demonstrators were assigned to each group, but in later years, as the number of tours multiplied considerably, special self-guide booklets were prepared for teachers so that each group could carry out its assignment by itself but with exhibit demonstrators on call to offer explanations as needed. The young visitors always have been urged to bring their lunches, which they deposit in huge wicker baskets inside the main entrance and at the tour's end find in an allotted space in the "picnic room." "The Museum," Gillet wrote in the *Elementary School Journal* some months after the tour program began, "makes every effort to cooperate with the schools. Its purpose is to supplement classroom instruction and enlarge ideas and understandings. Teacher and demonstrator may work together as the class is conducted through a section; they may help each other in stimulating and guiding thinking toward increased comprehension."

Each year saw an increase in the number of school-age visitors who came in chartered buses, many of them to return on weekends with parents or friends. By 1949, a peak of 133,008 in 3,276 such groups was reached, with the largest attendance (62,402) from elementary schools, and while the greatest percentage of all such visitors came from the Chicago area, there always were others from the rest of Illinois, Indiana, Wisconsin, and Michigan, and special student groups, although not as part of the school tour program, from Colorado, New York, and France. These figures were part of a total attendance for that year that Lohr described in his report to the trustees as "the most astounding record in the history of the Museum." Nearly every month had seen a great increase over that of the same month in 1948—

113,348 in October against 87,827 the previous October, 151,674 in November against 99,744, and on December 4, a new all-time mark for a single day of 24,902, nearly five thousand higher than the previous record. For the entire year, the mark had not only reached 1,500,000 but exceeded it substantially, for a new record of 1,666,454. And with this Lohr had other happy tidings: The average length of stay, now reckoned at slightly over three hours, was twelve times greater than in 1939. In spite of increased operating costs for labor and materials, the cost for each visitor hour had gone down from seventy-seven cents in 1939 to ten cents. And the budget for 1950 contemplated expenditures of $522,000, with anticipated income, unlike the situation a few short years back, at that precise figure.

3.

Before the year was out, the Museum acquired another exhibit that had little to do with science or industry but would bring to the Museum hundreds of thousands who might otherwise not have been lured there.

At a dinner to open the 1949 edition of the Chicago Railroad Fair, Lohr found himself seated next to Homer Hargrave, a wealthy Chicago stockbroker, and Mrs. Hargrave, a vivacious woman known to millions of moviegoers of an earlier generation as Colleen Moore, the bobbed-hair symbol of the "flapper era" of the 1920s. In the course of their conversation, she told him about her famous half-million-dollar dollhouse, which had been touring the world for fourteen years in behalf of children's charities and which she hoped soon to lend or give to an institution for display.

"Why not the Museum of Science and Industry?" asked Lohr.

"Science and industry?!" countered Mrs. Hargrave. "What

on earth would a dollhouse do there with all those gadgets and big machines?"

Lohr proceeded quickly to explain that while the main purpose of the Museum was to show the relationships of science to industry and the application of both to improved production and better ways of life, he was not averse to including displays that were purely for joy and entertainment—and might entice visitors not unduly interested in scientific and industrial exhibits. He cited "Yesterday's Main Street," with its nickelodeon and an arcade where visitors could be photographed in a setting of the 1890s. He assured Mrs. Hargrave that not only would her dollhouse be safe in the Museum but that it would become one of the places most alluring attractions. "They will come to see the dollhouse," he told her, "and perhaps a little science will rub off on them."

Mrs. Hargrave's dollhouse had a long and interesting history. When she was only two years old, her father, Charles Morrison, constructed the first of several dollhouses she would own for the many dolls she possessed. At seven she received from her father a gilt box one inch square, inside of which lay a tiny dictionary with words so minute that they could be read only with the magnifying glass on the cover of the box. With this as a starter, she began to collect miniature objects of all kinds, and by the time she was a major star in Hollywood, she had a storage cabinet filled with them. To house these treasures, she was urged by her father to hire an architect and artists to build and furnish a home for them. Horace Jackson, a set designer for major movie companies, created it in the form of a castle that was built after nearly seven years of painstaking effort by some seven hundred artists and specialists under supervision of Miss Moore's father, a technician named Jerry Rouleau, and Harold Grieve, a decorator employed by many of the prime Hollywood families. This remarkable creation, measuring nine feet square and standing twelve feet high, with two hundred movable parts and its own electrical system and running water in bathrooms and kitchen, went on display in 1935 in R. H. Macy's department store in New York, in the first stop on a national tour to raise money for crippled children. Mrs. James D. Roosevelt, President Roosevelt's mother, was present to slip the golden cornerstone into its proper place, and New York's former governor Alfred E. Smith was on hand to make appropriate remarks.

Over the next decade and more, in nearly three hundred cities, millions of men, women, and children paid to see the wee wonders in Colleen Moore's Fairy Castle, as it came to be called. Jackson had designed it so that, unlike other famous dollhouses, it represented no particular architectural period; "Early Fairy," Grieve replied whenever he was asked what period the furniture exemplified. From every part of the world its owner gathered incredibly small antiques, part of some two hundred thousand individual items. These included chairs, fireplaces, tables, beds, and fountains, all especially constructed on a scale of one inch to a foot, and jade and ivory work from China, tapestries and glass from Italy, art and sculpture from France, wood carvings from Germany. Replete with turrets, steeples, dungeons, and gardens, the castle perched on a ragged precipice resembling a medieval mountain. Four hundred tiny electric bulbs screwed into sockets no larger than pinheads furnished light. Fountains fed by water tanks on the turrets sparkled and splashed in the kitchen, bathrooms, and the Garden of Aladdin, where a tiny feathered nightingale perched on a lavender glass tree sang in full-throated style, weeping willows really wept, grapevines bore clusters of pearls, and tiny flowers bloomed only in moonlight. Inside the castle's eleven rooms were treasures of an amazing variety amid furnishings of gold, silver, and ivory. On the walls of the Great Hall were paintings of such fictional characters as Snow White and Alice of Wonderland fame, and portraits of the actress herself in an Alice-blue gown she had worn in one of her biggest hits, *Irene*, and of such comic-strip characters as George Mc-Manus' Jiggs and Percy Crosby's Skippy and, inevitably, of Walt Disney's Mickey and Minnie Mouse as King and Queen of Hearts. A chandelier, strung with diamonds and other gems worth fifty thousand dollars, hung from the drawing-room ceiling decorated with misty clouds that drifted against a sea-blue sky. The room's floor, made in China in nine months, was of rose quartz inlaid with silver and gold. In the imaginative library the fireplace was in the form of a fish net, and in its folds were two mermaids and a Father Neptune whose face, on close inspection, turned out to be that of Wallace Beery, the famed seriocomic movie actor. On miniature shelves stood a collection of unusually rare books, one of a kind, bound in leather on whose covers were embossed in gold such names as Irvin S. Cobb, Sinclair Lewis, F. Scott Fitzgerald, Booth Tarkington, John Steinbeck, Carl Van Vechten, Fannie Hurst, Adela Rogers St. Johns, Edna Ferber, Joseph Hergesheimer, Elinor Glyn, Robinson Jeffers, Willa Cather, and other writers Mrs. Hargrave had come to know in her Hollywood years; she had ordered these miniature books made with blank pages, and on these the authors had inscribed sentences from their books.

Another room was a replica of King Arthur's dining hall, featuring the renowned Round Table with each knight's chair and heraldic shield in place and dining service of solid gold, and in the adjoining kitchen was a teaspoon-sized cookbook with recipes contributed by world-famous chefs and a complete dinner service of Royal Doulton china bearing the crest of Mary, the Queen Mother of England. On the second floor were bedrooms of the Sleeping Princess and the Prince—the first in mother-of-pearl and gold, the second in bronze, and both with furnishings of gold and ivory—and the Treasure Room, guarded by the figure of Ali Baba and holding quantities of such fairy-tale items as antique charms, love potions in jeweled decanters, enchanted rings, and the strange devices of magicians and sorcerers.

Lohr's argument persuaded Mrs. Hargrave, and she consented to lend the Fairy Castle for at least a year, with a proviso for annual renewals if the relationship proved mutually agreeable. Rather rapidly, construction was completed at the rear of the Museum of a special room illuminated by twinkling stars and soft moonlight, and by October all was ready. The Fairy Castle was immensely popular from the start, and this initial popularity has never slackened over the years. Mrs. Hargrave always has taken a strong interest in the exhibit, making frequent visits and occasionally adding such new objects as a sliver of the True Cross given her by Clare Booth Luce, who had received it from Pope Pius XII when she had her first audience with him as the new American ambassador to Italy, and a set of Early American pewter mugs whose handles had been carved from wood recovered from World War II debris of the bombed section of Westminster Abbey.

And to those who ponder the appropriateness of a lavish dollhouse, however unique and fascinating, near old-style fire-fighting devices and views in the Microworld Theater of the tiniest known living organisms and models of nuclear engines and portrayals of radiation at work, Lohr's explanation, in answer to his own question at a board meeting after the opening, still seems quite valid. "It may prove to be one of the best exhibits that we have," he said. "A hundred thousand youngsters a year will come to see it who would not walk across the street to the best science exhibit. It is located in the far reaches of the building, and in order to get to it many other exhibits will have to be passed, and it's certain that some of them will intrigue the interest of those who had been motivated only to see the Fairy Castle—and perhaps their interest will be intrigued sufficiently to come back for further study. . . . In many fields, propaganda is directed to those already convinced because they are the ones with whom there has been contact and hence are known. The difficulty is in reaching those who are not known and those who have not yet made up their minds. There are few more important functions of the Museum than to stimulate and encourage an interest in young people in science and industry, especially those who have no inkling of their existence and therefore have no incentive to learn about either."

CHAPTER XII

THE AMAZING U-505

One day in 1949 Lohr was visited by the Reverend John
Ireland Gallery, pastor of St. Cecilia's Church, on the city's
South Side. The priest expressed his enthusiasm over exhibits he had seen that morning, then asked, "How would
you like to have a German submarine?"

Lohr was immediately interested, recalling that a World
War I submarine had been one of the stellar attractions at
the Deutsches Museum. He asked for more details, and his
visitor eagerly furnished them.

The submarine he had in mind, said Father Gallery, had
been captured at sea six years earlier by a task force headed
by one of his three Navy-officer brothers, Daniel V. Gallery,
then a captain and now an admiral. It was the *U-505*, a
920-ton, 252-foot raider that, after its commissioning on August 26, 1941, had preyed on allied shipping in the Atlantic
Ocean with considerable success. As commander of the
United States Fleet Air Base at Reykjavik, Iceland, after
America's entry into World War II, Gallery had sent his
planes to hunt and sink Nazi submarines amid icebergs,
sleet, and gales. In January 1944 he was given command of
the *Guadalcanal*, a baby aircraft carrier he promptly nick-
named "Can Do" and which, with five destroyer escorts,
Pillsbury, Pope, Flaherty, Chatelain, and *Jenks,* constituted

a "hunter-killer" task force assigned to seek out and destroy more enemy submarines. After sinking two U-boats in the Azores, Gallery set as his task force's objective the capture rather than the sinking of the next submarine it encountered so that valuable documents and equipment could be seized.

On the Sunday morning of June 4, 1944, the U-505 was spotted by sonar submerged 150 miles off Cape Blanco on the coast of French West Africa and tracked down. Four depth changes were sent its way by the *Chatelain*, two considerably off the mark, the others close enough to spin the submarine around. Crew members of the U-505 rushed to the area where Commander Harald Lange and his officers were having Sunday dinner. They cried out that a portion of the craft had been ripped open and that water was seeping in. Lange gave the order to surface. As the U-505 did so and its officers and crew clambered onto its decks, one of the destroyers, seven hundred yards away, fired a round of small-caliber shells to prevent the manning of deck guns and scuttling of the submarine. One man in the sub crew of fifty-four was killed, and several, including the commander, were wounded. Lange then ordered the opening of an eight-inch scuttling port, and as water began to flood the craft, he called out, "All hands out of the boat! Sink the ship!" As the Germans dropped into the sea and boarded small life rafts, Lange, believing that the craft was sinking, cried, "Men, give three cheers for our ship!"

Then came a command from Gallery that had not been given in 129 years by an American naval officer in combat: "Away all boarding parties!"

Motor whaleboats immediately set out from two of the destroyers with Lieutenant Albert R. David of the *Pillsbury* in charge. David and seven *Pillsbury* crewmen boarded the submarine. Some seized code books and other important documents. Motor Machinist's Mate Zenon B. Lukosius replaced the screw-down plate on the scuttling porthole. And

David and two crew members, Arthur W. Knispel and Stanley E. Wdowiak, risked their lives to enter the darkened hull to defuse demolition charges. All this took ten harrowing minutes, after which the submarine's batteries, gave out, the motors stopped, and the craft sank lower. On Gallery's order, the *Pillsbury* moved in to take the *U-505* in tow. But the destroyer came so close that the submarine's diving planes, jutting to the sides, slashed into it and damaged it so severely that its two main compartments were flooded. Gallery then sent the *Guadalcanal* after the quarry, and, with Commander Earl Trosino in charge, a boarding party successfully snared it.

For three days the submarine, dubbed by Gallery "Can do, Junior," remained linked to the carrier. Then it was transferred to the Navy tug *Abnaki* and towed not to the nearest port, Dakar—that city was infested with German spies and it was imperative that the capture remain a top secret—but seventeen hundred miles to Port Royal Bay, Bermuda. The three thousand members of Gallery's task force were sworn to secrecy, the Germans were led to believe that the *U-505* had been sunk, and in the months that followed, the information yielded by the capture—the first enemy ship seized on the high seas since the USS *Peacock* took possession of the British *Nautilus* in 1815—proved immensely valuable. Found aboard were five acoustic torpedoes, which, by sound alone, had been able to hunt down and hit Allied ships. To counter these, noisemaking devices were now developed so that acoustic torpedoes would be directed to them rather than to the ships by which they were towed. Captured code books furnished innumerable clues that enabled Allies to intercept and unscramble enemy radio messages in directing operations against U-boats for the eleven months of the remainder of the conflict. In the entire war, 781 U-boats were sunk, and of these, 290 were sent to the bottom in the period after the *U-505*'s capture. For the feat, Gallery's task force received a Presidential Unit Citation, with a Congressional Medal of Honor for David and Navy Crosses for Knispel and Wdowiak and a Silver Star for Lukosius. As for the sub itself, it had finally been brought to the Navy yard at Portsmouth, New Hampshire, where it now lay rusting and evidently doomed to the scrap heap.

2.

Lohr's interest was considerably aroused as he learned more about the historic capture and the possibility of acquiring the craft for the Museum. At the urging of the *Tribune*'s publisher Colonel Robert R. McCormick, Senator C. Wayland Brooks introduced a bill authorizing the removal of the *U-505* to Chicago, but there remained the problem of who would pay the two hundred thousand dollars estimated to be needed for transporting and rehabilitating the craft. The Navy rejected any suggestion that it assume this expense—some high officers recommended that the submarine be taken out to sea and sunk—and Lohr was hardly prepared to commit the Museum to so large a sum. So the project languished, except for occasional statements by Naval Reserve officers in Chicago about the desirability of bringing the submarine to the city either for training purposes or as a memorial to local Navy men who had lost their lives in the war.

In the summer of 1952, after Gallery had been promoted to rear admiral and appointed chief of the Navy's anti-submarine division, Edward Dunne Corboy, director of the Irish Fellowship Club, urged the city council "to enlist the support of public-spirited citizens in making Chicago the permanent home of the captured vessel as a monument to a past accomplishment and a reminder of future problems." A resolution to this effect was passed by the aldermen the following March after Gallery, newly assigned as chief of reservists at the Naval Air Station in suburban Glenview, warned that unless quick action were taken, the Navy might soon sell the craft for scrap metal. Colonel McCormick volunteered to assume part of the towing costs by using one or more of the ships of his newsprint fleet plying the Great Lakes between Chicago and the newspaper's mills in Canada, but the Treasury Department ruled against this on the ground that federal regulations prohibited vessels of Canadian registry, as the *Tribune's* were, to tow craft of American registry in United States waters.

In April 1953 Mayor Martin Kennelly appointed a forty-six-man *U-505* Committee to raise money to carry out the project from start to finish. Most of the rest of the year was devoted to an intense campaign for such funds—the goal was set at $221,000, with forty thousand dollars needed as soon as possible to pay for dry-docking and emergency repairs—and innumerable studies by a corps of volunteer engineers and assorted experts headed by Seth M. Gooder, a man of experience in moving large structures, on how best to transfer the vessel by way of the St. Lawrence River and the Great Lakes to its final berth at the Museum. When, on several occasions, suggestions were made that perhaps a more logical place might be Grant Park, on the eastern edge of the downtown district, or near the Naval Armory in Lake Michigan at the foot of Randolph Street, Lohr was quick to plead his cause; in a letter to Ralph A. Bard, the Chicago businessman and former Navy Undersecretary who was honorary chairman of the *U-505* Committee, he cited the great rise in attendance at the Museum, promised a display that would enable visitors to enter the submarine and see its actual workings, and predicted that it would equal in public interest the famous coal mine.

Contributions came from businessmen and industrialists, from thousands of citizens, many of them war veterans, and from other sources ranging from the Electric Boat Division of the General Dynamics Corporation, builders of the new, atom-powered *Nautilus* submarine, to the Chicago Building

Trades Council comprising 135 labor unions. Gallery won a five dollar bet from Janet Irwin, Lohr's secretary, that he could get a five hundred dollar contribution from Samuel Cardinal Stritch, head of the vast Chicago Catholic archdiocese, but sent back her check with a note reading, "I discussed this bet with my brother, Father Gallery, and he said it was a miracle that we got that $500, and since it is immoral to bet on miracles, I am returning your check." Miss Irwin promptly contributed the five dollars to the fund. From Herman Wouk, author of the best-selling *The Caine Mutiny* came a five hundred dollar check with a letter attached: "The U-505 will do something dear to my heart, something I tried to do as well as I could in my small way in the 'Mutiny'—never to allow Americans to forget that there were once Nazis, and that they were driven from the face of the earth with the help of the armed forces of America."

There were those who thought otherwise and inveighed against the whole idea in letters to the newspapers. Carl Stockholm, cochairman with Robert Crown of the fund-raising committee, replied that the exhibit would be "a constant reminder of the splendid heroism of our Navy men who gave their lives to maintain our freedoms . . . and a splendid educational exhibit showing the intricate machinery necessary to wage warfare under the seas." Gallery responded with similar sentiments, admitting that in a purely material sense the exhibit would be of no practical value but that emotionally and historically it would benefit the community. "In this day and age, too many of us judge every question on the basis of 'What is there in it for me?' There is nothing much in this project for any individual—no professional fund raisers are being employed in it. But there's a great deal for the community and the future. When a country becomes so absorbed in its present that it forgets its heroic past, then its future is in danger."

When contributions were slow in coming, editorialists reminded readers that Texans had made a shrine of the old battleship *Texas,* now moored permanently in San Jacinto State Park, near Houston, and Governor William Stratton intoned, "More than a million dollars was contributed by citizens of the Lone Star State for this project. Surely Illinoisans will respond to this opportunity to bring to our state a living memorial which marks one of the Navy's victories at sea." The Milwaukee *Sentinel,* noting the lagging fund drive, proposed bringing the U-boat to its city. Crown responded, "We won't surrender the *U-505* to Milwaukee or to anyone else," and a new flurry of letters in the newspapers was touched off when Patrick Shane, a truly chauvinistic Chicagoan, reacted to the newspaper's proposal with "Tut, tut, Milwaukee. They seem to be having delusions of grandeur. . . . The only reason anyone ever hears of that town is that some bottling works puts up billboards all over the country claiming that their pop has made the village famous. . . . And where would they put the sub even if they got it? Chicago has a number of suitable sites, including the world-famous Museum of Science and Industry. In Milwaukee it would overshadow the whole town like Ringling Brothers circus at a whistle stop." Shane was replied to in kind, Duane Becker advising him to "take a short trip and see a really progressive city" and Dorothy Tedrom characterizing Chicago as a city "that can only brag of rotten slums and politicians who are so crooked that I'll bet they use oversized corkscrews to sleep on" and Rupert Kuhn proposing that Milwaukee take the submarine and sent it to the bottom of the Milwaukee River, so that "our good German friends up there would not have a public monument to remind them of the late Adolf Hitler who was a disgrace to the German race."

Amid the clamor, the fund drive picked up speed, paced by a heightened publicity campaign spurred by Jack Foster, a Naval Reserve officer and first-rate newspaper reporter turned equally adept public-relations expert. By the end of the year, nearly half the total amount had been raised, and in the next four months, while finishing touches were being made on the *U-505* in its Portsmouth berth before setting out on its 2,750-mile trip to an offshore position in Lake Michigan near the Museum, more cash contributions were received along with scores of offers from construction and engineering firms of services and materials for the task of beaching the vessel after its arrival. To the $175,000 collected, the Museum trustees voted to spend up to twenty-five thousand dollars in connection with displaying the *U-505* properly, and on March 9, 1954, in a Pentagon ceremony attended by MacMaster, Stockholm, Crown, and Senator Everett M. Dirksen, Navy Secretary Robert B. Anderson officially transferred title of ownership of the naval prize to the institution which had promised to care for it in good and proper style.

3.

The final voyage of the rust-crusted *U-505* began the following May 15 after a delay caused by high winds. Slowly it made its way up the Atlantic Coast toward the St. Lawrence River, towed by the tug *Pauline L. Moran,* and then continued through the river's twenty-six locks with only six inches of clearance on each side and into Lake Ontario, first of the three Great Lakes it would traverse before reaching its ultimate destination. For most of the trip from Montreal, the *Airbanas,* a yacht owned by U. A. Sanabria, a Chicago television-set manufacturer, accompanied the craft. At Detroit, Gallery came aboard for the last leg of the journey, and in Milwaukee the submarine tied up for a one-week stay. With fireboats spouting streams of water into the air and with an escort of the training destroyer *Daniel Joy* and two submarine chasers and a flotilla of a hundred private yachts, the captured submarine arrived in Chicago on June 26, remaining for the weekend at the Michigan

Avenue Bridge for the benefit of sightseers, and then was towed south to be tied up at a pier in the Calumet River shipyards.

A veteran in his highly specialized profession, who, in nearly forty years before his retirement in 1951 had supervised the moving of structures as heavy as ten thousand tons and the underpinning of hundreds of buildings, Seth Gooder had planned for this complex engineering venture with great care and intricate detail. To lighten the job of bringing the *U-505* overland, thirty thousand gallons of fuel oil and ninety-six tons of iron ballast in its keel were removed from it. It was then placed on a floating dry dock and mounted on a specially designed undercarriage that could ride on steel rollers and rails and towed to the Lake Michigan shore, eight hundred feet from its permanent resting place. A steel pier jutting fifty feet into the lake was constructed, and a 325-foot channel was dredged nine feet below the water line to enable the dry dock to float up to the pier. The first step of the delicate operation, involving some forty engineers and workmen, lasted nearly four hours on the warm night of August 13, when the dry dock was gently nudged by two tugs toward the pier and then sunk until the submarine was level with the tracks on the pier, after which it was pulled ashore on other tracks by cables powered by a winch on a truck two hundred feet away. For two weeks or more, visitors to the nearby beaches and to Jackson Park and the Museum came to stare at the vessel as it lay on the beach. Motorists were startled and amused by a nearby sign: "Submarine Crossing. Drive Carefully." There now remained the final step, and at 7 P.M. on September 2, the scene illuminated by floodlights from two Fire Department light wagons and with fifteen thousand people watching, that arduously slow process began. Lake Shore Drive, separating the beach from the Museum grounds, was closed to all automobile traffic as fifty yellow-helmeted laborers helped to move the vessel slowly on its way, first on rails and then on wooden rollers that resembled giant rolling pins, with cables tugging it inch by inch. By midnight the U-505 had covered half the distance, and by 4:15 o'clock in the morning it had cleared the roadway and lay ready to be pulled into position, in the next four days, into three cradles of reinforced concrete beside the east wall of the Museum.

4.

For the formal dedication on September 25 Lohr had asked Admiral Chester W. Nimitz, commander of the American naval forces in the Pacific during the war, to be the main speaker. The white-haired admiral replied that he would be out of the country on that day but suggested, "Dan Gallery should be the guest of honor at this dedication. I feel strongly that no one senior to Gallery from the Armed Services should be present to detract from the glory and attention that is Gallery's." No glory seeker, Gallery told Lohr, "I'm flattered, but this is one of the few subjects on which I would differ with Admiral Nimitz. Under no circumstances should this become a personal glorification project for me. So far as I'm concerned, the more senior people we have on hand for the ceremony, the merrier!"

Telecast over the Columbia Broadcasting System network, the dedication was a colorful event, with Navy jet planes roaring overhead and a Navy dirigible hovering nearby, a choir of sixty-two Naval Air Corps cadets from Pensacola, Florida, the band from the Great Lakes Naval Training Station, and an honor guard of thirty Marines, and two Navy patrol craft escorts which fired a salute when Arthur Godfrey, the television/radio star and a Naval Reserve commander, presented Fleet Admiral William F. Halsey. To the assembled dignitaries, nine crewmen from Gallery's original hunter-killer force, and a crowd of twenty thousand,

Halsey said, "The U-505 will always serve as a reminder of a Godless way of life that puts might over right and makes of its citizens slaves of the state. As a permanent exhibit at the Museum, it will always remind the world that Americans pray for peace and hate to fight, but that we believe in our way of life and are willing and capable of defending ourselves against any aggressors."

Lines of visitors started forming at once on the day after the ceremonies—nearly thirty thousand paid twenty-five cents each in the first three weeks—although much needed to be done to rehabilitate and refit the submarine and put it in working order. Lohr, remarking after his first thorough examination of the interior, "This is still a stinking tub," instituted a wide search for a vast variety of items—diesel-engine valves and tachometers, radio-room gear, sonar and radar equipment, weapons, electric heaters, lifejackets, officer and sailor caps, uniforms and insignia, life rafts, a periscope—that had been removed by the Navy for study or by souvenir hunters during the submarine's long stay in the Portsmouth Navy Yard. He sent letters to a hundred American and German navy men asking for leads on needed materials and also dispatched Sterling Ruston, the Museum's registrar, to search in Navy warehouses for whatever could prove useful. Bit by bit, the response came. After a visit from MacMaster, the giant Maschinenfabrik Augsburg-Nürnberg in Augsburg, Germany, sent—without cost—fuel-injection needle valves, water thermometers, admission handwheels, and other parts essential to the operation of the diesel engines. For a year, two engineers from the electromotive division of the General Motors Corporation, William Becker and Rod Wallis, worked nights to bring the engines alive again, even persuading their company to donate an air compressor required to turn over the engines. From varied sources here and in Germany came German radio tubes, officers' all-leather uniforms, submariners' caps, a crash-dive Klaxon, short-wave radio equipment, storage batteries, switches, fuse boxes, and the original periscope, regained from the Navy Department's curator. A dozen former German submariners living in Chicago volunteered their services for whatever tasks were needed in the rehabilitation; one of them, Hans Decker, who had served on the U-505, went to work for the Museum as a maintenance man on the submarine. Illinois Bell Telephone technicians restored the intercommunication system, and staff members of the University of Chicago's Institute for Nuclear Studies reconstructed the submarine's compass.

One of the largest caches of important equipment resulted from a visit to the submarine in September 1955 of Carl T. Milner, a civilian research engineer at the Navy Underwater Research Laboratory, after which he asked to see Lohr. "When the Navy stripped the U-505," he told him, "I was told to junk a lot of the stuff, but it seemed too valuable for that, so I stored it in my basement. It's there now, and I'll be glad to send it to you." What came from Milner's basement was two thousand pounds of irreplaceable electronic sound-detection and radio equipment. Delighted with this find, Lohr received permission from Captain Edward L. Fahy, director of the Groton Laboratory, to have Milner assigned to the submarine for a week to help with the installation. After Milner returned to his job, he made two more contributions—an additional three thousand pounds of U-505 parts collected from other technicians at the laboratory and a tape recording for the sonar room of typical underwater sounds of fish, freighters, and warships.

By late 1956, nearly two years after the dedication, Lohr was pleased to announce that he considered the U-505 fully restored except for some less crucial items, one of which became available in 1965 when the West German Defense Ministry dispatched a rack of five carbines of the kind used by the U-505 and other German submarines when boarding halted merchantment or in guarding captured enemy prisoners.

5.

The *U-505* has never lost its allure as one of the Museum's banner attractions. Since the beginning, an average of ten thousand visitors a week have passed through it, to make their way along the narrow steel platform running its length, stooping to avoid being bumped by overhanging pipes and compartment doorways, pausing to examine the assorted devices and accouterments, to peer through empty torpedo tubes and examine the control room, conning tower, and diesel-engine room and stare at the thirty-four crewmen's bunks neatly made up in traditional blue gingham sheets and pillowcases and at the spare quarters once occupied by Commander Lange. In 1964, when the submarine welcomed its five-millionth guest, Lange, by now executive director of a Hamburg fruit-import co-operative, was himself a visitor, musing over the seizure ("I'm glad those days are over"), expressing pleasure at the vessel's condition ("It's good to see she's still in good shape"), and receiving from Gallery, retired and writing books, his binoculars taken at the time of capture. "It was a matter of war," said Gallery, "and we were professionals who had a job to do."

In later years, at the request of various German officials and Americans of German descent who hoped thereby to erase the Hitler taint and because of the help received from German firms and individuals in the submarine's restoration, Lohr agreed to remove "Nazi" from the bronze commemorative plaque affixed to the submarine and substitute "German." But unchanged was other wording on the plaque: "This prize of war is dedicated to the memory of the Americans who went down to unmarked ocean graves helping to win victory at sea."

CHAPTER XIII

ALWAYS CHANGING

The decade of the 1950s was marked by important events and activity at the Museum in addition to the acquisition of the *U-505*, although without doubt that prize produced a mass of local and national publicity that prompted a considerable rise in attendance. The period began with only three thousand more than the 1949 record mark of 1,666,454, then continued to climb at a faster pace—1,853,693 in 1951 and 2,157,430 in 1952—and, in the three years when hundreds of news stories appeared about the submarine from the start of the fund campaign to its placement in the concrete cradles and its first full year of exhibition, 2,255,735 in 1953, 2,655,128 in 1954 and 2,795,120 in 1955. All sorts of records were established in the period, and Lohr, invariably and with pride, reported them to his trustees; the minutes for the October 1951 meeting included a typical entry: "The Chairman said that in one month the Museum had broken records for the Largest Month, the Largest Week, the Largest Single Day, the Largest Sunday, and the Largest Weekday attendance. During the first two days of September, 1951, 51,781 persons visited the Museum, while in 1940 the attendance for the entire month of September was only 39,854. On Sunday, September 2, there were 27,705, on Labor Day 24,076, and Thursday, August 16, made a weekday record of 12,978. The Chairman said that during the month of August there were 293,096 visitors. He also presented a record of Out of State License Plates recorded on three test days during August. These showed a preponderance of out of state visitors during the month and indicated a widespread visitation from all the States of the Union and the Provinces of Canada."

These individual and annual records would continue to be bettered as the years went on, and the trustees sought several times to offer tangible recognition of such progress by raising Lohr's annual compensation by ten thousand dollars, but not until 1967 did he agree to accept a salary of thirty-five thousand dollars. For Lohr there was no magic or mystery about the reasons for the Museum's progress and fame. He had charted its way in all the formal and informal discussions in the weeks after he had taken on the difficult assignment and in his notes and memos and speeches. He had never doubted that his pragmatic approach to problems would bring desired results, and he had not swerved from his essential goals: To make the Museum a place of fascination for all people, whatever the extent of their formal schooling, and to meld entertainment and education so skillfully as to render, pleasurably and painlessly, instruction and inspiration for further learning, to create a virtual people's palace of learning, where surprise and innovation were the accepted norms in an always changing setting.

At the core of this success were many new exhibits and a wide range of activities—all, of course, so systematically publicized by Hildebrand and by Fred Ashley, who succeeded him in 1956, that forty magazine articles and three thousand newspaper stories were not an unusual annual yield—that seemingly never seemed to slacken. The 1940s had been a decade of confronting and conquering crises, of enduring necessary austerity, and of consolidating gains. The 1950s were a time for growth and diversification and the accumulation of new attractions to lure more and more visitors a first time—and a second and a third and endlessly.

2.

Of all the industrial exhibitors in the Museum, the Illinois Bell Telephone Company had been the oldest and most steadfast in extending the scope of its exhibits to reflect new trends in telephonic communications. Its display at A Century of Progress was shifted to the Museum in 1935, and changes had been made every few years to reflect developments in the industry. In the busy and bustling 1950s, it maintained its innovative pace. In 1951 one of the devices introduced was an instant playback of a caller's voice and an oscilloscope on which sound waves were shown in color. At this exhibit's opening, Lohr paid special tribute to the company which had been such a persistent exhibitor since the Museum's earliest days. Dutifully he acknowledged its high-grade scientific and technological aspects, but stressed even more the quality he himself considered so essential an ingredient of his own management of the Museum—an enlightened public-relations policy. "The sands of American industrial history are strewn," he said, "with the bleached bones of technically sound business enterprises which have failed." The new exhibit would have a life expectancy of about five years, and in this time, he predicted, at least 7,500,000 people would visit it: "They will give it not merely a cursory glance as they might a publication or advertisement, but will spend 10, 15, 20 minutes or more in it. They will enjoy it and they will learn from it. And I believe that educators will agree that when the student enjoys the teaching process a great step has been made toward causing him to learn and to retain the information he has acquired."

Lohr's prediction was correct on two counts: the constant need for revisions and the estimate of numbers of visitors.

Late in 1956 several new sections were added, featuring the first public showing of a pair of greatly acclaimed innovations in communications: a pea-sized transistor then being used experimentally in a national toll-call dialing program and a solar battery by means of which sunlight was converted into electricity to supply power to telephone lines. As ever, visitors could learn the workings of the revolutionary transistor by participating instead of merely observing. With the flick of a switch, music from the transistor was transmitted into a radio receiver and into a battery of radio headsets that enabled several spectators to listen to the demonstrations simultaneously. New, too, were a section of the 2,250-mile transatlantic telephone cable, the first actual voice link between North America and Europe, which had been put into regular service that September—and capable of handling three times the traffic that had until then been carried by radiotelephone—and telephone hand sets that enabled visitors to hear transcribed playbacks of the initial conversation carried on the cable.

Popular from the start and through periodic revisions, the Illinois Bell Telephone Company's exhibit, whether under its original title of "Your Telephone," or in conjunction with the Bell Telephone Laboratories, American Telephone and Telegraph Company, and the Western Electric Company as the current Hall of Communications, has continued to be a perennial crowd attracter and an effective institutional public-relations project. In an expansion of the company's space in 1963 to twelve thousand square feet and with its elements estimated to be worth $425,000, a new Bell Theater featured continuous demonstrations of electronic writing pens, machines that could "talk" to other machines, telegraph and data networks, and satellite communications. By this time John Glenn had made his historic flight into space, and one of the company's fifteen displays was a full-sized model of Telstar, the Bell Telephone System's experimental communications satellite. There were, in addition, an elec-

After his success as president of Chicago's Century of Progress Exposition, in 1933–34, Rufus C. Dawes was named the Museum's president.

Lenox R. Lohr, who came to the rescue of the Museum in 1940.

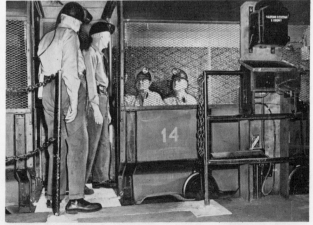

The Museum's famous coal mine, earliest and still one of its most popular attractions.

Crowds line the banks of the Chicago River in 1954 to watch the captured German submarine *U-505* being towed toward its permanent site at the Museum.

Among the first visitors at the Museum's opening in 1933 were (left) Caroline Kreusser, daughter of its director, Mrs. Julius Rosenwald, and Tommy Goodkind, one of Mrs. Rosenwald's grandchildren.

Major Lohr and Daniel MacMaster greet Dr. and Mrs. Clarence Davis, of Bloomington, Indiana, and their sons. Mrs. Davis was the fifty-millionth visitor to the Museum, in 1964.

England's Queen Elizabeth and Prince Philip flank Major Lohr during their visit to the Museum.

Museum of Science & Industry

King Frederick II of Denmark inspects the U-505.

Chicago Photographers

Pics Chicago

Maurice Chevalier was a constant Museum visitor during every professional appearance in Chicago.

Colleen Moore Hargrave shows India's Prime Minister Jawaharlal Nehru her famous Fairy Castle.

Vyacheslav Molotov, at the peak of his power as the Soviet Union's foreign minister, listens to Major Lohr expound aspects of American scientific and industrial achievement.

The great gospel singer Mahalia Jackson, seen here with Daniel MacMaster, was a frequent Museum visitor.

tric larynx developed by company scientists to facilitate speech by the voiceless, and "Telefun Town," in which animated puppets amusingly illustrated various uses of solar energy and the research and work required to produce telephones, and where children, by pushing buttons, heard the voices of Walt Disney's Mickey Mouse and Donald Duck talk about how to use telephones or sent signals to a miniature Telstar. In subsequent years, constant additions have included the Picturephone, by which a visitor can make calls to Disneyland and see the person at the other end, "sensicall" telephones enabling deaf persons to understand incoming calls by seeing coded light flashes that replace vocal sounds, a "teleclass" communications setup by which a teacher can instruct disabled pupils in many locations miles away, a "school-to-home" amplified speaker system in both home and school classroom enabling the student to question a teacher directly, and a variety of modern and futuristic electronic devices that permit activities ranging from holding one call while talking to someone else without the need for a second line to a system of abbreviated dialing whereby certain numbers called frequently might be reached by using only three digits.

3.

Late in 1952 there went on display what was described in detailed press releases as "the largest heart in the world." This was a precisely modeled, three-dimensional heart standing fourteen feet high through which a visitor might walk and examine simulated muscles and valves of the heart chambers and hear a heartbeat magnified a dozen times. It was the most striking item in an exhibit presented by the Chicago Heart Association for the prime purpose of clearly and articulately explaining to laymen all aspects of heart disease—and, hopefully, to teach what might be done to prevent it. Toward the latter aim, at one end of the exhibit was placed another beating heart, this time in the form of a pool of light where a visitor could check his pulse against the exhibit's, then ascend a short ramp and again check the pulse to show how much additional work the heart performs even in such a slight effort. "Hercules Heart, the Mighty Muscle" stressed the amazing efficiency of the heart as it pumped a tiny hand car on a toy railroad track to transmit such information as that in a lifetime the heart actually outlasts seven powerful automobiles each driven for ten years for a hundred thousand miles and that the energy exerted by the human heart in an average lifetime is sufficient to pull a train loaded with 226 tons of freight from Chicago to New York in seven and a half days. To show the heart's pumping action was one of the most complex electrical mechanisms ever constructed in the Museum, an enormous, sectioned heart, that, by means of changing lights, appeared to contract and relax as it pushed blood—the flow indicated by lights— through its chambers.

This exhibit, produced by the University of Illinois's professional colleges in collaboration with the association, replaced most of an earlier one dealing with structure and functions of the vital organ and a variety of adjacent medical displays (an old-style dental office, an exhibit showing the nervous system, dioramas on medical discovery and progress). It, in turn, was considerably revised in the 1960s to introduce a number of new elements. Considered by authorities the most extensive display of the heart and blood systems ever assembled, it features new techniques facilitating the replacement of diseased or damaged blood vessels, the introduction of nylon tubes into the heart for surgical diagnoses, displays in which buttons pushed by visitors illustrate in sequence the heart's anatomy and enlarged cross sections, a transparent plastic reproduction of the upper part of the human body thrice its normal size and, by a network of bright lights, clearly showing the entire circulatory system and animals' hearts descending in size from that of an elephant, as large as a basketball, to a hummingbird's, so tiny that it can be seen only through the built-in magnifying glass above it.

Another in the series of exhibits that concerned itself primarily with health was Swift & Company's "Food for Life" presentation, introduced in 1954 to portray the whole range of man's knowledge of foods for plants, animals, and human beings. Charts, colorful illustrations, dioramas, a miniature farm plot in which such garden and field crops as alfalfa, green beans, and tomatoes flourished under artificial light, a kitchen with realistic trappings right down to table settings —these and more all contributed to the exhibit's authenticity.

But the most appealing attractions then and later have been the live baby pigs, lambs, and other farm animals in a special nursery supervised by a trained animal husbandman and fed a diet scientifically balanced by Swift nutritionists, especially the one hundred baby chicks and ducklings that hatch each day in spectators' full view in two big, glass-walled incubators complete with custom-built thermostat and heating controls. Some visitors, especially those who are city-bred, have been known to spend hours at the incubator, staring down at the baby chicks as they push through their first openings in the shells until they tumble out of their broken eggs and stagger about on wobbly legs. A sign on the incubator gives assurance that the decrepit appearance of the newly born chicks and the apparent inability to walk are both natural and that in due time they will be sturdy. Occasionally the routine is varied, as in 1963, when the incubators were used for hatching bobwhite quail.

As in other exhibits first introduced in the 1950s, "Food for Life" has undergone revisions. One of the most interesting was the establishment in 1965 of a Consumer Research Center, where an average of one thousand persons each week were tested as to their preferences in varieties of foods from hot dogs to peanut butter. Out of these, say company officials, emerged valuable information on public likes and dislikes. They also gave the meat-packing firm clues on more effective packaging and advertising messages.

Still another medically based exhibit, opened in 1955, was Abbott Laboratories' complex but graphically instructive presentation called "The Conquest of Pain." As the name implies, it was designed to delineate the character of pain and the ability to control it in treatment and in surgery. Still a popular attraction, at its entrance stands an eight-foot plastic figure of a man with all nerves traced; appropriately, it is across the way from the fourteen-foot heart. The intricate system of how a feeling of pain is received and transmitted is made clear to the visitor who touches a dummy hot plate, at which the plastic man touches another, thereby tracing the course of the pain message by a string of flashing lights from hand to brain to muscles controlling the arm. The history of anesthesia is delineated in a telephone narration—from the earliest uses of opium in alcohol through chloroform to modern drugs, in which the exhibit's sponsor is among the industry's leaders as the maker of Pentothal and Nembutal—as the visitor looks through a forward-slanting glass wall into a life-sized amphitheater at a tableau of a typical operation. In another section, different kinds of anesthesia can be administered to an anatomical model, and visitors learn, too, what anesthesiologists do to control a patient's pain and keep him alive, the uses of nerve-blocking chemicals, intravenous agents, and inhalation of gases, and methods of providing mechanical breathing.

4.

The opening, on the night of a heavy snowstorm, of a major exhibit sponsored by the International Business Machines Corporation—complete with a gala holiday banquet at which IBM's president, Thomas A. Watson, Jr., and Dr.

Detlev Bronk, president of the National Academy of Sciences, spoke—was the highlight of the Christmas season in 1956. In its original form and in almost completely revised form in 1961 this extensive exhibit, first called "The World of Numbers" and later "Mathematica—The World of Numbers and Beyond," has been one of the Museum's most ingenious.

More than two dozen displays of devices complex and simple carried out the basic motif of showing the application, in manifold ways, of the principles of mathematics. A major feature was the cycloramic staging of Project Sage, a computerized air defense system in which, by simply lifting a telephone, one put into operation a simulated air attack by enemy bombers, and the subsequent relaying of information to the computers at Air Defense Command Centers, where the Sage computer calculated, in a millionth of a second, the speed, course, and altitude of the approaching fleet, thereby giving jet interceptors, Nike missiles, and coastal anti-aircraft batteries exact knowledge of the enemy's direction and precise points of interception. A host of items signifying man's eternal search for mechanical means of speeding the solution of mathematical problems were laid out: a giant abacus so built that the push of a lever afforded simplified operation; the seventeenth-century computing rods invented by John Napier, the Scottish authority on military science and coinventor of modern logarithms; Grillet's pocket calculator of 1678; Pascal's first mechanical calculating machine, of 1642; and, as the climax to the array, a model of IBM's most recent electronic data-processing machine complete with translucent wall diagram of the intricate operations and a recording of a step-by-step explanation of how problems are presented to it, how they are solved, and how answers emerge. Adjoining the computer, animated panels with electronic tubes flicking off and on further explained ways of the marvelous invention, from the use of the binary number system to the storage of facts and figures as magnetized dots on magnetic tapes, disks, and drums. Hanging from the ceiling were models of a geodesic dome and an earth satellite. Other structures—jet aircraft, Nike missiles, atomic power plants—in which mathematics played a crucial part were pictured in a mural. Interspersed were a number of games to test one's mathematical knowledge and abilities or to attempt to illustrate problems in algebra, trigonometry, and other basic mathematical processes, and, as stated in comprehensive press releases, "to lift mathematics out of a prosaic, textbook atmosphere and present it as an active, interesting subject."

In a new guise the 1961 IBM show was even more fantastic to look at, a collection of oddly shaped apparatus and whirling lights and objects in a unique setting, the entire complex created by the world-famed designer Charles Eames and his wife, Ray. The Eameses spent a year in research, read innumerable books on mathematics, and traveled from England to Japan for source material.

"Mathematica" has long since ranked as one of the Museum's most dramatic areas, combining effectively the principles enunciated by Lohr and presenting an initial impression upon entering it of some Midway, part-carnival, part-magicland, part-science laboratory. At the entrance a chief allurement is a twelve-foot-high wall of hollow glass resembling a giant pinball machine; inside, 7,500 plastic balls constantly cascade from the ceiling into grooves to demonstrate a probability curve. In a machine nearby, to dramatize multiplication tables, a visitor presses a number, which is instantly multiplied by another, then squared and cubed by the lights of a huge, 512-bulb cube. A few feet away, to bring sharply to view principles of motion and gravitation, a spectator pulls a plunger and launches a miniature sphere that orbits around a center as a planet does around the sun. The giant abacus and the other models illustrating break-throughs to new mathematical knowledge are in the central area. To one side is a "peep show" whose colorful movies offer simplified words to explain fundamental mathematical concepts. From the ceiling hang placards with quotations from famous mathematicians (Weierstrass: "It is true a mathematician who is not something of a poet will never be a perfect mathematician"). A sixty-foot-wide History Wall documents in pictures and text contributions of the world's leading creative mathematicians during the past eight hundred years, and on a Mathematical Images Wall is a profusion of natural and man-made objects visually impressive and mathematically significant—tornadoes, sea shells, snowflakes, curves, tree rings, honeycombs, fingerprints, X-ray photographs of a chambered nautilus, nebulae, starfish, and crystals. Of the latter, Eames was especially proud. "What brought it about," he told interviewers, "was that we found that we hadn't touched nearly enough of the material that is mathematics. We decided to draw on those aspects of mathematics that had a vivid imagery to which the uninitiated would respond, imagery that the initiated would also find meaningful and appropriate."

And additions and revisions continue to be made. In 1967 a display of mirrors of distortion usually found in amusement parks was set up to afford fun and laughter—and also offer a lesson or two about topology, the special branch of geometry concerned with ways in which surfaces can be bent, pulled, stretched, and twisted from one shape to another and yet remain basically the same. To the History Wall —in response to periodic suggestions from mathematicians visiting the Museum—the names of those responsible for "mathematical reading tables" were installed to illustrate anecdotes and lore in the lives of history's best-known mathematicians. Unchanged and underscoring one of the purposes of the entire exhibit was the statement by Albert Einstein that adorned the History Wall: "How can it be that mathematics, a product of human thought independent of experience, is so admirably adapted to the objects of reality?"

5.

In the thriving decade were other additions, some offering sheer fun, others pleasure with instruction, others informal education.

High spectator interest in the several old-fashioned automobiles long parked along "Yesterday's Main Street" led to organization of a section in 1955 titled "Cars of Yesteryear," in which fourteen vehicles, restored to pristine condition in the Museum shops and capable of being driven under their own power, were ranged along two rows. Lohr himself stayed at the Museum past closing hours on many nights to help such experts as Jack Brause, who had worked on Stanley Steamers, and Rube Delaunty, once a chauffeur for John G. Shedd, late president of Marshall Field and Company, in their task of restoring the old cars. Representatives of various eras of motor development were the 1896 two-passenger runabout of the gas-engine type invented by Karl Benz, with a chain drive from its three-horsepower engine to its light, wire-spoke wheels; a 1904–5 Stevens-Duryea in horse-carriage mode; a 1906 Cadillac touring car and a 1912 model with Charles F. Kettering's revolutionary electric starter-generator; three Henry Ford creations, the 1908 and 1914 touring cars and the 1924 coupé, still with the somber, squarish Model-T appearance; the 1909 Gleason, with high, buggy-type wheels that its manufacturers thought would have special appeal for farmers; and the 1911 custom-modeled Simplex, with long wheelbase and oversized wheels. To give spectators a better time sense, such contemporary accouterments were displayed as a Regina music box playing melodies from perforations on a metal disk, an Edison phonograph with its cylindrical wax record, a late-nineteenth-century wall telephone, and a foot-powered sewing machine.

And throughout the Museum a plethora of others, permanent or temporary:

Eight companies combined to establish the first of several exhibits dealing with the petroleum industry: four scale models of drilling rigs and, against a panoramic mural of a huge scarlet sun beaming yellow spokes of energy to growing vegetation and a spotlight aimed at a huge slab of yellow porous rock whose crevices were filled with the liquid crude-oil residue of organic matter, dioramas of progress since the first American oil well was sunk, in Titusville, Pennsylvania, by Colonel Edwin T. Drake in 1859.

The first exhibit of color television, in 1950, at whose opening David Sarnoff offered a sage prediction: "Television may well determine a future President of the United States. He'll have to be photogenic, wear the right necktie and smile pleasantly. But most of all the candidate will have to reflect in the television screen whatever sincerity is in him."

A model of the artificial earth satellite that was launched into outer space during the 1957 geophysical year.

"Americade," a visual presentation by the National Association of Manufacturers envisioning changes in the country's rapidly growing economy.

The United States Atomic Energy Commission's "Atoms for Peace" exhibit in 1957, made up of fully equipped miniatures of most of the nation's atomic-research centers.

"Tale of a Tub," the Maytag Company's version of how America's women had, as the press release from the washing-machine manufacturer put it, "been freed from most of the household drudgery borne by their grandmothers."

Louise Gardner's collection of more than five hundred dolls from thirty-four European countries, the Near and Far East, the Caribbean Islands, and North and South America.

The growth of American commercial aviation as depicted by United Air Lines, and the history of flight as presented by the Civil Aeronautics Administration.

Latest scientific weapons devised by the Army, and "Seapower," the Navy's pictorial report on atomic and supersonic projects.

The Upjohn Company's "Human Cell" exhibit, displaying mankind's smallest living organisms magnified more than a million times.

"A World of Hardwoods," comprising replicas of mighty oak trees and animated models of a sawmill and plywood plant and an earnest message to spectators to help conserve forests.

"Magic in Motion," the University of Chicago's demonstration to explain basic laws of physics through the use of nontechnical language and ordinary devices such as bowling balls and toy trains to drive home deeply technical lessons.

6.

Supplementing the manifold exhibits were special events of all kinds: A lecture series each spring and fall, concerts by military bands and symphony orchestras on the outer pavilion in the summer, colorful programs commemorating national holidays, and a wide variety of special short-term displays, among them an exhibit of Latin American architecture and a series of Spanish plays as part of a Festival of the Americas, a Panorama of Canadian Progress, a display of award winners in the Diamonds International competition, a Health Fair with exhibits ranging from the model of an operating room for open-heart surgery to an electroencephalograph to detect various brain disorders. Meetings of important scientific and medical groups proliferated. One that was especially gratifying to Lohr was the observance in 1952 by the American Society of Engineers of the hundredth anniversary of its founding, an eleven-day meeting attended by hundreds of representatives of mechanical, chemical, metallurgical, electrical, and other engineering sciences. That occasion was marked, too, by the laying of the edifice's cornerstone, a ceremony neglected back in 1893; into a one-ton granite block were sealed a packet of radioactive material, penicillin, hydrogen, oxygen, a metal alloy, Oriental lotus seeds, several types of viruses and bacteria, and a specially constructed clock that would tick but once a year.

Events designed principally for the young were especially successful in the wake of a Youth Hobby Fair that had been instituted under auspices of the Rotary Club in 1947. The *Tribune*'s "Miracle of Books" began in 1953 and continued for over fifteen years, displaying each time three thousand books for youthful readers and presenting programs, plays, and speeches by authors. Of great and lasting import have been the Student Science Fairs that started in 1951 and, ever larger and more comprehensive, have prevailed ever since. The initial one was arranged under auspices of the Chicago High School Physics Teachers Association to stimulate interest in science—in the preceding twenty years there had been a noticeable drop in enrollment in science classes above the tenth grade—and show accomplishments of scientifically minded high school students. The timing was propitious, for in the years ahead public interest soared in such scientific developments as space travel and beneficial adaptations of atomic energy. The young exhibitors reflected this heightened interest. What began as an experiment with some one hundred student-built projects illustrating basic scientific principles grew swiftly into an annual event of considerable importance, supported financially by some fifty business firms. Rules set up later required that prospective exhibitors enter regional showings in school areas so that the best might be selected for the four-day display and judging for excellence by a jury comprising scientists, technicians, and teachers. Awards include medals, United States Savings Bonds, and college scholarships. In 1972, at the twenty-

second annual fair, winners of scholarships and prizes total-
ing nearly two hundred thousand dollars represented the
most original, well-organized, and scientifically important
among many thousands from all over the city and reflected
again youthful interest in scientific matters of concern to
the world community. Twenty of the 246 finalists dealt with
such ecological problems as the effects of pollutants on
plants, animals, and humans, and another twenty-five with
environmental hazards and perils.

7.

At the decade's end, Lohr could report more substantial
progress than ever before in the Museum's history. Revenues of $1,192,023 totaled nearly ninety-five thousand dol-
lars more than expenses, and this excess had been spent in expanding the parking lot, enlarging the children's picnic
room, and improving the building's outside lighting; the latter was done not only for aesthetic purposes but to provide
tourists a better opportunity to take photographs of the imposing structure. Beyond the material gains, he was pleased
to reflect on the great number of scientific and medical exhibits that had been installed in these years and the enlargement of opportunities for mass education—and, of course,
maintenance of increasing attendance records. "With the
great expansion of our school population in the face of a serious teacher shortage," he stated in his 1959 report, "the Museum's educational facilities are becoming more and more
important. This has been accentuated by the increased public interest in science and technological progress. Almost
every time some new scientific headline is featured by the
newspapers or over our radio and TV media, visitor attendance at the Museum spurts." The figures, of course, bore him
out. There had been an anticipated decrease from the all-
time high in 1955—first full year of the *U-505* exhibit—of

2,795,120. But the spiral remained high in the remaining years of the productive decade—2,250,077 in 1956, 2,306,681 in 1957, 2,504,391 in 1958, 2,547,231 in 1959—to top all other museums of comparable size and scope anywhere in the world.

CHAPTER XIV

QUEENS, KINGS, AND MOLOTOV

With the burgeoning fame of the Museum, it became a top-flight attraction for notables, whatever their interests, during short or long stays in Chicago. Steady publicity, tourists' guides, reports by travel writers, word-of-mouth enthusiasm all served to implant the Museum in the minds of those coming to Chicago on other business as a place in which to spend time. Moreover, by the 1950s the United States State Department began to include a stop there on the itineraries of distinguished foreign visitors, and most of the local consuls, working closely each year with the Museum in preparing for the well-attended and well-publicized "Christmas Around the World" pageantry, invariably persuaded important guests from their native lands to take advantage of Lohr's invitation to lunch and a special tour. In the first year of that decade, for one example, distinguished visitors ranged from India's prime minister, Jawaharlal Nehru, and Pakistan's prime minister, Liaquat Ali Khan, to Arturo Toscanini, renewing an acquaintance with Lohr that had started in the days of Lohr's presidency of the National Broadcasting Company, and James Melton, the operatic tenor, and in later years from Willy Brandt, when he was mayor of West Berlin, to Manuel Prado, President of Peru. In 1958 the first of many surveys was made to determine the areas from which all visitors came. For six days in July fifty thousand of the 350,000 who passed through the imposing front doors were asked where they lived; the results indicated an interesting diversity—2,787 cities and 230 small towns in the United States and fifty-seven foreign countries. This was, of course, during the vacation season, when close to 80 per cent of visitors were from outside metropolitan Chicago, a percentage invariably reversed during the winter months.

Museum lore is replete with recollections of visitors who remain memorable for a vast variety of reasons, some of them significant in their uniqueness, such as the entire formally clad wedding party that toured for two hours because of a delay in a planned reception at the University of Chicago's Rockefeller Memorial Chapel or enthusiasts who have paid the expenses of tours by visitors who might not otherwise have been able to afford them. One benevolent visitor/host was Jay Ostrander, an English teacher in a Goodrich, Michigan, high school who by 1959 had brought twenty-three groups of youngsters to the Museum in chartered buses for five-day visits. Pressed by reporters for reasons for his munificence (he also paid hotel and food bills) for the latest band of thirty-nine sophomores from a small-town agricultural school, he explained, "I'm a bachelor making about $5,000 a year. I have a car, I spend $10 a week on a room, I do my own cooking, I don't care for vacations in Hawaii or Europe. What else would I do with my money?"

A less humble but memorable visitor was Billy Rose, the diminutive, voluble Broadway showman. On a seven-hour stay in 1955, with not even a pause for lunch, Rose strode about the building, dropping tart remarks while taking shorthand notes. His favorites were the Bell Telephone System's multifarious devices ("These people know how to do things. I never saw a telephone show that wasn't good"), the "Harvester Farm" and "Yesterday's Main Street" ("That nickelodeon is the best thing here"), Colleen Moore's Fairy Castle ("Marvelous! I'd like to get it away from you!")

Swift's "Food for Life" ("Superb! Things are personal and that's what I know and am interested in"), and the fourteen-foot heart ("To walk through that heart is the best idea I've ever heard of, it's personal because everybody has a heart").

Rose frankly admitted that he was seeking ideas for an extravagant project—never realized—that would cost $150,000,-000, a fifty-story complex of exhibition halls and studios atop Pennsylvania Station in New York to be called the Palace of Progress, in which scientific exhibits similar to the Museum's not only would be included but where products would be advertised and sold.

2.

With their entourages of aides, security officers, and translators, and reporters and photographers, royal visitors invariably come to the Museum during their stays in Chicago.

Belgium's King Baudouin found himself entranced by the playback of his voice in the Hall of Communications, and Japan's Crown Prince Akihito and his wife, Princess Michiko, spent hours at the Museum, she particularly delighted by the enchanted garden in Colleen Moore's Fairy Castle and he greatly interested in a temporary exhibit showing how jets, turbo-props, and other power plants might someday be adapted for land transportation, and so intrigued by the idea of starting a similar museum in his country that he directed three of his aides to spend a hundred dollars assembling three sets of all Museum postcards, color slides, pamphlets, and books about the *U-505* and the Fairy Castle. King Frederik and Queen Ingrid of Denmark, before their tour, were feted on the "Harvester Farm" with a rural lunch of chicken and dumplings, homemade bread, side dishes of strawberry preserves, cottage cheese, tomato wedges, and pickled beets, and, for dessert, pumpkin pie. Waiters wore blue overalls, checked shirts, red bandannas, and straw hats,

and waitresses featured sunshade bonnets and crisp check-
ered pinafores. The monarch had never tasted pumpkin pie
before, but was so captivated that he first asked for a second
helping and then for a full second helping of the entire
luncheon.

The visit of royalty that produced extensive news coverage
was that of England's Queen Elizabeth and Prince Philip in
the summer of 1959, accompanied by local notables including Mayor Richard J. Daley and Governor William Stratton
and their wives. A photograph of the queen with Lohr at
her side as she spoke into a specially installed pink Princess
telephone to record her statement, "This is how I sound to
others on the telephone," for instant playback, appeared in
hundreds of newspapers in the United States, Canada, and
Great Britain. Dozens of reporters faithfully relayed the information that Prince Philip asked innumerable questions of
MacMaster as he lingered over displays demonstrating diesel power, color television, internal-combustion engines,
wheels, brakes, and tires, that the Queen noticed the British
Spitfire fighter plane hanging from the ceiling, that she was
startled when a low "Moo" issued from the "Harvester
Farm's" mechanical cow, and that when she prepared to
leave—for an emergency visit to a local dentist because of a
painful toothache—she sighed and said to MacMaster, "I so
wish my children could have been here with me to see this
wonderful place."

3.

Of all the foreign visitors, among the most frequent and
persistent have been Russians, all intensely interested in
technical and scientific matters.

It started early in 1955, when Vyacheslav M. Molotov,
then the Soviet Union's foreign minister, and a large aggregation of aides were compelled to wait for several hours be-

tween trains on their way to San Francisco for the observance of the tenth anniversary of the founding of the United
Nations. After a tour of the lakefront and a stroll along Michigan Avenue, the party hired an automobile, and, without
advance notice to Lohr, drove to the Museum and inspected
only one attraction—the *U-505*. They then returned to the
train station to resume their journey westward. When Lohr
learned that Molotov would be stopping off in Chicago again
on the return trip, he sent him a telegram inviting him and
his aides to lunch so that he might show him the movie of
the *U-505's* capture and other Museum attractions.

Upon his arrival at North Western Station amid cheers
and jeers from a clamorous crowd of five hundred, Molotov
and his party headed directly for the Museum. After a roast-
beef lunch in a private dining room attended by, among
others, Major General John Homer, who had met Molotov
in Iceland in 1942 while the Russian was traveling incognito
as "Mr. Brown" from Moscow to Washington, Molotov expressed interest in a score of other exhibits. For three hours,
with Lohr at his side, he toured the Museum. He shook his
head in apparent wonderment at the Goodrich Rubber Company's exhibit in which a thirty-four-pound weight resembling a guillotine was raised thirty feet and then dropped on
an inflated tire with force equal to that of an automobile
hitting a curb at sixty miles an hour but with no injury to
the tire. Inevitably he heard a playback of his voice in the
Hall of Communications. At the Argonne National Laboratory's exhibit of the contrivance in which an operator,
shielded from lethal radioactivity, manipulated a robot to
perform various chores in a nuclear reactor, he asked whether
the exhibit was open to the public or restricted to special
guests. He appeared absorbed in studying the working model
of a boiling-water nuclear reactor in the Commonwealth
Edison Company's exhibit, in whose Electric Theater he
asked many questions about the production of light by a
mixture of various chemicals. He posed amiably for photog-

raphers—whose pictures, as in the case of the British royal visitors, received extremely wide publication except in *Pravda*—but balked genially at a suggestion that he don a linen duster and derby hat and pose in a 1902 automobile on "Yesterday's Main Street," where he stomped on the cobblestones and surveyed the old-fashioned trappings and asked, "Why should this be in a museum? You must have many streets like it in Chicago." Informed by Lohr that this was hardly so, Molotov shrugged and strode into the adjoining General Motors "Motorama," there to turn the crank of a 1912 Buick engine and observe transmission systems from the old-fashioned gearshift to the Dynaflow turbine drive. At lunch, Lohr had sought earnestly to explain to Molotov that one of the elements in the Museum's philosophy was to show the benefits of the free-enterprise system, and at this exhibit Molotov's interpreter, Anatoly Dobrijorian, translated aloud, at Lohr's suggestion, this inscription on a nearby panel: "Opportunity. America leads the world in producing more and better things for more people. America was settled by men and women in search of freedom and opportunity denied them in their homelands. Here they found freedom to worship according to their own individual beliefs and opportunity to develop land and resources for their own individual betterment."

Molotov departed for New York with a promise—never to be fulfilled, for he was soon deposed and shunted into obscurity—of returning one day to Chicago if only to spend more time at the Museum of Science and Industry. For all his ardor, his two stopovers were given the barest mention in *Pravda's* account of the delegation's travels. The newspaper reserved its highest praise for San Francisco ("Unusual beauty, cleanliness, and a certain freshness"), made meager mention of Chicagoans who had sent peace petitions to the United Nations' commemorative conference, and had harsh words for New York ("Filthy streets with hot and humid air, recalling a steam bath").

Despite *Pravda*'s lack of enthusiasm or journalistic inadequacies in reporting on Molotov's stay in Chicago, scores of other Russian visitors have since come to the Museum. In 1958, no fewer than twelve such groups came; they included plastics engineers, educators, and movie actors, directors, and technicians. Although most delegations have been amiable, a disagreeable flurry was raised in 1960, when D. S. Polyansky, a high-ranking Soviet Government official, insisted on cutting short the tour he and his twenty-five associates were making so that they could inspect steel mills and factories. Anatoly Gromyko, son of Foreign Minister Andrei Gromyko, and Nikolai I. Sergeyev, deputy minister for machine tools and instrumentation, led a group in 1966 that was reasonably impressed by major exhibits and, like typical visitors, found simple enjoyment in pushing buttons to work displays and watching movies at the nickelodeon.

In the past two decades inspection teams have come from Canada, Spain, Brazil, Australia, Israel, Puerto Rico, and Egypt to spend weeks or months with one purpose: to study the Museum of Science and Industry, ask hundreds of questions about its operations and economics, and return with plans for starting similar museums in their own countries.

Along with visits, a number of important foreign exhibits from Iron Curtain countries and other lands have been featured periodically in line with this country's cultural exchange program. As they do in the number of visiting delegations, the Soviets lead. Their first was a medical exhibit in 1961, with thirty tons of equipment including an ultrasonic diagnostic machine and "sleep machines" used in treatment for mental illness. Two years later four thousand volumes in technical fields were shown, and in 1970 an impressive "USSR Photo '70" featured twelve hundred photographs selected from some seventy thousand submitted on virtually every aspect of life and living in the Soviet Union—people of varied nationalities, sled-dog trains and locomotives, iron-covered church walls, skyscrapers, log stockades, snow-covered cabins and summer dachas, city streets and primitive farms, sports events, and historical reminders of past wars. Other foreign exhibits have included one from West Germany showing achievements in five hundred years of printing and German contributions to physics, medical science, and mathematics; a Romanian tapestry and textile show; a Polish Science Fair, with instruments and manuscripts dating from Copernicus to Madame Curie; a "Vienna Gloriosa/Creative Austria" display of innumerable aspects of that country's achievements in the arts, sciences, technology, and industry. A prime accolade was received on a visit by Leo Heuwing, then director of the Deutsches Museum, during one of the Student Science Fairs. So impressed was he that he carried the idea back with him to institute a similar project at the institution that had now, as he put it, "to learn from its pupil."

CHAPTER XV

MOVING WITH THE TIMES

As the Museum entered the 1960s all signs pointed to an
even greater surge of public interest and attendance. Increasingly, and indicative of its growing renown, it continued to play host, in addition to its multitudes of regular
and special visitors, to important conclaves dealing with
contemporary issues, typical of which, in the decade's initial
year, was the Second Annual Youth Conference on the
Atom, sponsored by foremost investor-owned public-utility
firms and attended by 250 prominent educators and 400
topflight science students, and a massive parley of leaders
from twenty-two nations in commerce, labor, and industry.
The Museum's financial health had never been more robust;
with splits in its Sears Roebuck and Co. stock and reasonable
success with other holdings, the value of its portfolio now
stood at over eleven million dollars and additional revenues
of some five hundred thousand dollars—approximating income from all sources in 1940—primarily from admissions
to the coal mine and the *U-505* and museum-tax revenues,
supplemented stock dividends handsomely. And honors
accrued to Lohr and the Museum. At the start of the
decade he received the coveted Oskar von Miller Medal,
named for the founder of the Deutsches Museum, and the
Museum a plaque from the West German Government—

the first of its kind ever given to an American institution —for its role "in making the public aware of the technological and scientific possibilities and challenges of our time and thus making an important contribution to the strengthening of the alertness of the free world." Later from the same source came the Commander's Cross of Order of Merit for Lohr as the only non-German member of the Deutsches Museum's advisory committee and from the University of Chicago the esteemed Rosenberger Medal, conferred only fifteen times since its inception in 1924 on recipients who included Frederick G. Banting, discoverer of insulin, the noted archaeologist James Henry Breasted, and Paul G. Hoffman, administrator of the Marshall Plan.

At this time, Lohr suffered the first of several heart attacks, each requiring that he reduce the pace of his activities periodically, although invariably after a period of recuperation and rest in his home in Tucson or his Evanston residence he renewed his duties with as much energy as he could muster.

No year passed in this period without important new exhibits, their aggregate value running as high as one million dollars in 1961 and $2,207,000 in 1962. Reflecting vital advances in the world of science, the United States Atomic Energy Commission's new nuclear-science exhibit, largely replacing the "Atoms for Peace" display, offered various dramatic features, including a cutaway model of the place beneath the University of Chicago's Stagg Field where in 1942 Enrico Fermi and his colleagues produced the world's first self-sustaining nuclear chain reaction, a cloud chamber for observing tracks of cosmic rays and other particles, and a manipulator cell to show the use of mechanical "slave-arms" in handling radioactive materials. At the vortex of the Union Carbide Corporation's Hall of Elements was set a full-scale replica of a nuclear reactor, the Commonwealth Edison's scale model of its new nuclear power station in downstate Illinois. Other additions included a model of a Mercury space capsule built by the McDonnell Aircraft Corporation, a model of a working base and living quarters designed by the Republic Aviation Corporation for earth explorers of the moon, and the Hughes Aircraft Company's air-to-air missile, the Nuclear Falcon.

The Schwab Foundation sponsored a series of lectures for young visitors by Dr. Daniel Q. Posin, an ebullient and extremely entertaining physicist. Every talk by Posin was a dramatic performance. Lecturing about atomic reactors, Posin would bound about the stage, point to a large model of a reactor, and declaim: "Now why do they call this a materials-testing machine? Why? It is already making power. Isn't that enough? The radiations are coming out of the bars of uranium. They are heating up water. Steam—it is going through the pipes, driving wheels, making electricity, it is coming out. Everybody is happy! But the scientist wants to put something in there, through that hole some material, and see what it will do to the material while all that business is going on. . . . The crazy scientist always wants to know something new. The other business, the power—that is already known. He will leave that for the engineers to handle. So the scientist will poke maybe a bottle of iodine through that hole and leave it there for hours while the radiation is going on—brrrrrrm, brrrrrrm, brrrrrm." Then, wiggling all his fingers rapidly so that they looked like goldfish milling in shallow water, Posin expostulated colorfully on atomic fission. So well received were Posin's lectures—he also won numerous awards for his imaginative lectures on the Chicago educational television station, WTTW—that a Schwab Foundation trustee, Lazarus Krinsley, was moved to write to Lohr, "If all the donations made by the Schwab Foundation trustees are as worthy as the one to the Museum for these lectures, the trustees will not only have performed their obligations with excellent judgment but they have in my opinion done what Henry C. Schwab would have wanted done if he were here."

In the section devoted to transportation three famous trains were added. The first, in 1960, was the Burlington Pioneer Zephyr, progenitor of diesel-powered streamliners, and it was followed by the Santa Fe's 2903, another monarch of the rails, and in 1962 by the New York Central's historic 999, revered by railroad buffs everywhere for having been the first steam locomotive ever to have pulled a passenger train at more than a hundred miles an hour—specifically the Empire State Express 112.5 miles an hour on a trial run May 10, 1893, between Rochester and Buffalo prior to her official debut at the World's Columbian Exposition. Number 999, out of service for decades, had been exhibited at the 1948 Railroad Fair, and one of its ardent admirers had been the *Tribune*'s Colonel Robert R. McCormick. At the fair's conclusion he had rather firmly suggested that he would be pleased to have as a souvenir the 999's whistle. The publisher died in 1961, and in restoring the old locomotive to its original state Lohr recalled the gift, made proper inquiries of *Tribune* officials, and received the whistle, along with a check for $2,500 to help pay for the rehabilitation. (The *Tribune* has been a persistent supporter of the Museum since its infancy, and in 1962 the Robert McCormick Charitable Trust contributed a $150,000 permanent exhibit, "The Newspaper in America," delineating every aspect of the production of a daily newspaper from the moment news begins to flow into editorial offices until completed copies roll off the presses for placement on trucks and delivery to newsstands and readers' doorsteps and porches.) In the weeks after the presentation of the 999, Lohr was pleased to drive home the benefits of affiliation with the Museum in a report to the New York Central's president, Alfred E. Perlman. Emphasizing that industrial concerns, including railroads, customarily receive scant publicity on worthwhile accomplishments but headlines on wrecks, strikes, or investigations by government agencies, he computed the amount of space devoted to the acquisition on the basis of clippings received: 548 news items, seventy-five pictures, and one cartoon in publications with a collective circulation of 32,987,119. There would be more press notices, he predicted, and he concluded, "I doubt if the New York Central could have purchased this amount of paid advertising for the original cost of the 999."

2.

Largest of the new exhibits in the first half of the 1960s was "Showcase for Steel," comprising twenty-five different units tracing the full story of steel production from raw materials to finished products. Under the aegis of the American Iron and Steel Institute, this co-operative effort by most of the country's major steel companies represented a case study of the meticulous care and detailed planning involved in preparation of major exhibits.

Lohr had long yearned for such a coup. First steps toward attaining it had started in informal discussions with representatives of the United States Steel Corporation and Inland Steel Company early in the 1950s and had progressed, by January 1958, to a point where Daniel MacMaster was transmitting to officials of Hill and Knowlton, Inc., the steel industry's public-relations representative, masses of pertinent data about exhibit philosophy, attendance, length of stay, numbers and sizes of organized tour groups and the parts of the country and foreign lands they represented. Detail by detail—right down to the kinds of chairs and carpeting for the proposed exhibit—a proposal was hammered out over the next two years in conferences and correspondence by Museum staff members with Hill and Knowlton representatives and executives assigned to the project by participating steel companies. As the complex venture advanced, all copy for scripts was carefully checked, whether for recorded narratives about operations of blast furnaces, open hearths, and slabbing mills or for promotional movies ("The Steel Industry and Its People" and "Steel and America," with Walt Disney's Donald Duck tracing the growth of the steel industry) and others on such technical phases of production as temperature, resistance, tool steels, and ductility. Hundreds of letters, memos, drawings, and layouts for booklets passed from Chicago to New York and from the Museum to the Hill and Knowlton offices, with carbon copies of all crucial material to institute officials and to executives of the firms involved.

At a gala dinner on December 12 for 330 guests, the institute's chairman, Thomas F. Patton, president of the Republic Steel Corporation, described the exhibit, covering more than fifteen thousand square feet on two floors, as the largest of steel and steel products ever staged for public showing and stressed its value in improving public understanding of the industry—a goal devoutly needed in the wake of loud protests, including the opposition of President John F. Kennedy earlier that year over the efforts of some steelmakers to raise prices. And Dr. Lee A. Du Bridge, president of the California Institute of Technology, sounded a familiar theme but one always welcome to the ears of Lohr, MacMaster, and their associates: "In opening this exhibit and in all that it does, the Museum of Science and Industry is a foremost medium of public education."

From the outside of the building, its center doors flanked by steel color panels, through the rotunda and main entrance with a circular ramp supported by steel cables announcing the institute's sponsorship, and into and through the mezzanine and first floor, "Showcase for Steel" presented a dazzling array. Every phase of steelmaking, in color, sound, and action triggered by push buttons, was shown, starting with the unloading of an ore boat and carrying of raw materials by ore bridges to the stockpiles, and the further shifting of coke, limestone, and iron ore into position for use in measured quantities to be carried by skip car up a steep track and discharged into the top of the towering blast furnace. Visitors moving through the exhibit watched lights leap like molten metal in the open hearths and heard the roar of ingots as they rumbled through the rolling mill. In brightly hued color transparencies such products of finishing mills as sheet and tinplate, structural steel, rods and wire and pipes and tubing were seemingly produced by visitor-operator diagrams. Elsewhere were dozens of other steel products from tool-steel drill bits to reamers and cutters. Water fell from a sixteen-foot steel fountain into three shallow catch basins, and nearby was a seven-room Home for Steel, whose patio contained only steel garden furniture, barbecue equipment, and gardening tools, whose swimming-pool fence was of vinyl-coated steel and whose every room was crammed with steel cabinets, counters, utensils, and fixtures. Another section, devoted to the people of the steel industry, featured a film about the workday of typical steelworkers and game-type machines offering statistics to persuade watchers that the workers are among the safest and highest paid in any industry; at the exit the world's largest stainless-steel mural—seven feet high and twenty-eight feet long, in which its creator, Nikos Bel-Jon, had created his abstract concept of the future uses of steel— had as its center a steel-like figure stretching upward and outward to symbolize, as the artist told reporters, "the unlimited potential of steel through the unlimited vision of man."

The intricately detailed arrangements had evidently all been worthwhile. "Public reaction to the new exhibit," MacMaster informed John Mapes, Hill and Knowlton's chief executive, a week after the opening, "is simply tremendous. Everyone agrees that it is one of the outstanding exhibits in the Museum. The compliments to all who had anything to do with it are being bandied about at great length." Supplementing the ranks of thousands who walked through "Showcase for Steel" were groups of employees from the affiliated steel companies who came for special showings after the official closing hour, and MacMaster was quick to pass on detailed information to George Rose, the institute's secretary, as in the case of Inland Steel Night, when 7,357 came instead of an anticipated two thousand and consumed 1,872 cups of ice cream, 3,000 ice-cream bars, 1,600 cups of coffee, 5,400 doughnuts, and 4,320 cans of soda.

As with other permanent exhibits on which great care was lavished and which had basic interest, "Showcase for Steel" has retained its initial mass appeal. Improvements and additions continue to be made: models to portray such revolutionary technological changes as the blowing of oxygen at supersonic speeds into iron to blow out impurities; the continuous-casting process, by which molten steel is taken from furnaces and cast directly into slabs and billets; fantastic sculpture fashioned from hundreds of fine steel wires; and stainless-steel-mesh drapes in the Home of Steel. And since the start, a special exhibit committee of institute members has watched over the huge exhibit and conferred regularly to suggest further adjustments, changes, and new concepts to keep pace with shifts in one of the nation's most vital industries.

3.

There were other exhibits of interest in this period, and, as ever, their forms and purposes were diverse. After three years of planning and construction, Abbott Laboratories' $185,000 "Chemical Man" was installed, a unique portrayal of the molecular action responsible for creating and sustaining human life. A grant from the A. Montgomery Ward Foundation made possible "Ships Through the Ages," a striking collection of ship models from those of the Egyptians of 2800 B.C. to the most recent atom-powered vessels. An

1857 blacksmith shop, in earlier years a highly popular attraction, was refurbished for display near "Showcase for Steel" to compare metalworking methods of a century ago with today's, and at it stood Carl Johnson, a smith for over half a century, to hammer out miniature horseshoes and other souvenirs from bars of hot iron. Even a drag racing car, named the Chizler, first ever to be timed at two hundred miles an hour, was placed on view in the rotunda, with MacMaster explaining, "Anytime anything comes along that's new and technically interesting we want a display on it. When atomic energy came along we had a display on that. We think this drag racing car is technically interesting and important."

And there was misfortune. On the afternoon of January 15, 1963, with the temperature outside at 12 degrees below zero, fire broke out in the medical section and drove employees and some six hundred visitors into the frigid cold. Smoke spread rapidly to damage "Miracle of Growth" and the cancer and polio exhibits and poured down the stairwells into the rotunda. Fred Ashley, the Museum's kinetic public-relations director, bustled about, assuring newspaper reporters who had rushed to the Museum after extra alarms had been sounded that the firemen had the blaze under control and successfully persuading the city's four major radio stations to permit him to broadcast a complete but unexcited account of what had happened—"without any exaggerations or attempt at heroics," as he stated in his report to MacMaster. After the fire was put out, Ashley also prevailed on WTTW, the educational television station then housed in the Museum, to announce several times during that evening that the Museum would be ready to receive visitors next morning. This was possible because Museum staff members and workers spent most of the night securing the immediate services of construction crews, plasterers, and painters. Damage was estimated at $250,000, but all was covered by insurance, and in due time the damaged exhibits were restored and, in some cases, improved.

4.

By 1965 annual attendance was more than ten times that of the Museum's opening year: 3,044,307 visitors. It would never go below that figure in the decade as the combination, now so firmly set, of outstanding exhibits and steady publicity time and time again proved its merit.

The next few years continued to be marked by triumphs —and some rancor and sorrow. The triumphs were, as always, in new exhibits, most notably the Eastman Kodak Company's "This Is Photography," including among many items a "time machine" which a visitor could manipulate to select historical events preserved on film, high-powered lenses through which to peer at a microworld of color, pattern, and texture, and lensless cameras using laser beams, and "Atomsville, U.S.A.," a United States Atomic Energy Commission exhibit for children (doors less than five feet high, no grownups admitted) to operate small-sized mechanical hands for handling radioactive materials and to pump stationary bicycles that determined the amount of electricity they could generate in thirty seconds. New individual attendance marks were recorded: the sixty-millionth visitor on November 21, 1967, Marine Lance Corporal David Nelson of St. Cloud, Minnesota, who received a handshake from Lohr and MacMaster and a mahogany tray, and the largest single day's attendance, 49,362 on the following December 3, when "Christmas Around the World" was devoted to Polish customs in observance of the holiday.

One exhibit intrigued many, but grievously distressed others. For years Lohr had welcomed exhibits fashioned by various armed services to show everything from methods of preparing food for men in uniform to latest types of combat equipment. Weapons of all kinds, from the Davy Crockett atomic missile to the M-6o machine gun, appeared regularly in Army exhibits without expressed objection, and the Museum had received many Army awards of merit and achievement certificates. Early in March 1968, however, a group of clergymen and laymen appeared outside the Museum to protest a new Army exhibit featuring a Huey helicopter used in Viet Nam to flush out guerrilla forces. Visitors could sit in the helicopter and squeeze the trigger of an electronically controlled machine gun aimed at a mural of a countryside with several shacks such as might be found in a village compound, and an electric sign lit up if a hit was made. The protestors, contending that the exhibit encouraged warfare, carried signs reading "Don't Teach Your Child to Kill!" and "End the War in Viet Nam," although some reporters covering the event insisted they saw some of the younger ones, after handing their signs to fellow marchers, enter the Museum and head for the controversial helicopter to try their luck with the machine gun. Besides marching, the group staged a sit-in and also held several rather tense discussions with MacMaster in which they demanded that the exhibit be roped off because of what they described as the exhibit's "carnival spirit" and insisted on a meeting with the Museum trustees. MacMaster continued to meet with representatives of the demonstrators, and on May 19 the helicopter exhibit was roped off. That same week, there were no protests or demonstrations when an Air Force exhibit opened, in which visitors could make simulated flights over points of interest in the United States. Nor were there any similar incidents in connection with other military displays until late in 1971, when thirty-five members of the Vietnam Veterans Against the War handed out leaflets outside the Museum and presented a statement detailing Air Force bomb tonnage in Indochina; the demonstration was calm, with MacMaster drawing praise from John Musgrave, the group's leader, for permitting distribution of the leaflets and for his invitation to have coffee and rolls in two empty rooms behind the Air Force exhibit.

5.

All that spring of 1968 Lohr looked forward to the opening of a stellar exhibit devoted to petroleum. He had started negotiating for it early in 1966, and impetus had then been given his campaign with an unrestricted grant from the Standard Oil Company (Indiana) Foundation. Now, construction of what would be the world's largest petroleum exhibit encompassing all aspects of petroleum technology, from exploration for crude oil to retail sale of products, was almost complete. The opening was scheduled for May 28, and in the week before, Lohr and MacMaster made an inspection of the mass of ingenious devices and ideas that would tell a story whose intent was serious but also afforded fun: a simulated trip through the earth's strata with a "talking wall" to explain the journey and describe geological factors related to petroleum's discovery; an Exploration-Production Theater with a unique film that not only described drilling for oil wells but gave the illusion that an actual drilling bit bore through the ceiling to the stage; a Risk Tower with a game that reckoned the odds against finding oil and awarded winners a medal reading, "I struck oil at the Museum of Science and Industry"; an Involvement Wall, where visitors could get the feel of hundreds of substances made from petroleum; a two-story fractioning tower demonstrating how petroleum products from gasoline to asphalt could be produced from crude oil; an automobile-driving game to test skills and judgment; a forty-eight-hundred-pound steel bearing that, unlubricated, was virtually immovable but could be easily shifted by a child when supported on a thin film of oil; a tableau of the use of petrochemicals in everyday living, and a community of animals in which scampering gerbils subsisted on a diet of protein and water produced entirely from petroleum.

As at so many previous important openings, a festive dinner was held in the central court of the Museum on the night of May 28, with welcoming comments by MacMaster, an invocation by Dr. Jerald C. Brauer, dean of the University of Chicago Divinity School, formal presentation of the exhibit by the foundation's chairman, John E. Swearingen, ("I can think of no more fitting home for it than here in one of the great museums of the world") and an unusually brief acceptance speech by Lohr. Swearingen then rose to present the main speaker, Illinois's junior senator, Charles Percy.

Unnoticed during the introduction of Percy was Lohr's quiet departure. As he sat down after making his reply to Swearingen, he was stricken with severe chest pains. Recognizing the symptoms of another heart attack, he quietly eased himself out of his chair and walked slowly through the shadows of the vast room toward his office, with Mrs. Lohr and Janet Irwin close behind. Lohr sat quietly while Miss Irwin summoned his chauffeur, and the two women went with him to Billings Memorial Hospital, on the southern edge of the University of Chicago campus. On arrival there, only fifteen minutes after he had slipped away from his place at the speakers' table, Lohr was dead at seventy-six.

There were expected eulogies: "A great loss to the people of Chicago," said Mayor Daley. "Chicago has lost one of its most useful citizens," stated the *Tribune*, citing not only Lohr's Museum triumphs and his credo of mass education but his innumerable civic activities, most notably chairmanships of the Metropolitan Fair and Exposition Authority, creating McCormick Place, the Illinois Commission on Higher Education, and the drive to raise funds for the Jane Addams Memorial Fund to preserve the original Hull

House on the new Chicago Circle campus of the University of Illinois. The *Daily News* saw him as a great communicator, with his living monument the Museum, which the editorialist described as "a continuing marvel of practical public education." The *Sun-Times* lamented the passing of "one of Chicago's finest and most dedicated citizens," and the *American* called him "the engineer with imagination" and, like the others, enumerated his substantial contributions to the city and its people. It remained for MacMaster to make pertinent personal comment in a letter to a Standard Oil official: "Major Lohr said that he never wanted to retire. If he had to go, I think he would have chosen just what happened."

CHAPTER XVI

THE PEOPLE'S MUSEUM

Trained in virtually every detail by the man he considered his "professional father" to take over the Museum's topmost post, Daniel MacMaster was named Lohr's successor as president. Before and since becoming director in 1951, MacMaster was a true disciple, hewing to the fundamental theories and philosophies enunciated by Lohr for nearly three decades. Like Lohr, he saw the Museum as an institution not devoted to the static cataloguing of history. In an interview with a *Daily News* writer, Michaela Williams, who described him as "a delightfully urbane and genial man, a perfect blend of pin-stripe, in sync with his enormous, clubby wood and leather office," MacMaster enunciated anew the nature of the Museum: "We are not a repository of things. Our object is to tell the basic story, show the process of its development and its application. Things aren't sacred to us. In fact, we are constantly renewing. Ten per cent of the exhibits are changed every year. There is always something new." Like Lohr, he was a steadfast exponent of the theory of the Museum as a medium of mass education: "Contrary to the methods of formal education, we overwhelm the person with information. As Marshall McLuhan has pointed out, a child doesn't learn in a linear way. All his senses are open to a barrage of information from which he has the ability to choose. Take learning to speak. There is nothing didactic about the way a child learns to speak. In fact, it is completely chaotic, and yet somehow he learns. The same with walking. It's a tremendous thing. He learns from immersion and participation, which is similar to our non-formal communication method here." He re-emphasized Lohr's concept of the Museum of Science and Industry as genuinely a people's museum: "Unlike formal education, no one is compelled to come here. People come here only if they want to. It is our function to make them want to come, and to serve them in the most democratic sense."

As director of the Museum, MacMaster had worked more closely with Lohr than any other official in charting and creating much of the progress made in ensuing years. He also had engaged in extracurricular activities of varied kinds, from the presidency of his suburb's school board and membership on the citizens' committee of the University of Illinois to service as a trustee of institutions ranging from the Chicago Chamber Orchestra Association to the Hyde Park Bank and Trust Company. He received various civilian-service awards from the Army and the Navy and such decorations as the Golden Cross of the Royal Order of Phoenix from King Paul of Greece and the Officer's Cross of Polonia Restituta from the Polish Government. But his primary interest, as it has been from the day he first went to work there as a guide in the summer of 1933, is the Museum. Always an early riser, he is a compulsive worker; a favorite phrase often used by him in speeches he enjoys making to student groups was from the German, "Arbeit macht das leben süss [Work makes life sweet]." And he now concentrates all efforts not only on maintaining the Museum's status as the city's well-proven foremost tourist attraction but to enhancing its values and extending its impact.

2.

In so doing, he has swerved from some of Lohr's established practices.

One area in which he instituted immediate changes was in the relationship with the Museum's trustees. When Lohr was selected in the dismal days of 1940 to head the institution and pull it back from what appeared to be the brink of extinction, he saw himself as a designated trustee appointed to a specific task which he would carry out to the best of his abilities without burdening the members of the Museum board with details. Consequently, most of the regular board meetings were cut and dried—except for the early ones, when Dr. Philip Fox's stubborn refusal to resign had to be discussed at vexatious length. In Lohr's Army-style opinion, the board members' primary functions were to approve or disapprove his management of the institution and to decide from time to time on what percentage of Sears Roebuck and Co. stock ought to be diverted to other investments.

Board members were invited to attend the Museum often, and a number of them made it a special point to do so. Occasionally a trustee offered suggestions about Museum procedures that proved beneficial. One came from Philip Clarke early in the 1950s, when he asked if it might be possible to keep the Museum open on some nights so that he could hold a dinner and tour for officers of his bank. The first of these was so successful that special dinners—not only connected with the opening of major exhibits but on other occasions—became standard practice, one of the most memorable being an eight-course banquet for fifty guests affiliated with United Air Lines, with each course prepared by an airline "super-chef."

Beyond this, however, board members hardly ever participated in detailed affairs of the Museum, nor did they get to know department heads and their functions unless Lohr found it necessary to have important actions involving such Museum officials approved. This method of dealing in strict echelon style had obviously worked to good effect, but MacMaster is more gregarious than his predecessor, and shortly after assuming the presidency he instituted a series of presentations of his prime aides at meetings to tell about themselves, their functions, and their responsibilities.

Consequently, starting that August and continuing at almost every meeting, board members met and heard from, among others, Carl Dude, the business manager, who relayed manifold details about all aspects of his job, from the issuance of some thirteen thousand payroll checks annually to over-all supervision of the eight dining rooms with annual sales of nearly eight hundred thousand dollars and net revenues of over $125,000; from Dr. Noble J. Puffer, former Cook County superintendent of schools, who as educational supervisor was responsible for maintaining the high rate of visitors from schools and allied groups (invariably one-sixth or more of total attendance) and supervising the training of guide-lecturers recruited from among high school seniors, college undergraduates and graduate students, and active and retired school and college teachers; from architect Olaf C. Harringer, manager of exhibits in every aspect from the development and supervision of design to their maintenance; and from Bernice M. Martin, operations manager, who had begun as a guide-lecturer and had succeeded Martha McGrew on her retirement in 1958. Reports were issued to board members periodically on a wide array of subjects, from details of Museum maintenance ("We use 200 gallons of glass cleaning solution, three and one-half tons of soap and 350 gallons of floor wax annually") to expenditures by visitors at the Museum Mart.

3.

Another way in which MacMaster has gone beyond the limits set by Lohr is the heightened courting of special visitors to the Museum. Although Lohr played well the role of host for guests, whose presence often produced large amounts of publicity not only in the city but sometimes, as in the case of Queen Elizabeth and Molotov, throughout the country, he actually took scant pleasure in this part of his job, especially in his final years, after he suffered heart attacks and was not in robust health. Like the good Army officer he was, Lohr carried out these duties manfully, conducting tours, presiding at lunches, and officiating at dinners held at the start of important exhibits or at other functions. But MacMaster had far greater relish for these occasions, and in subsequent years the list of special visitors has expanded considerably.

This has been especially true in the case of foreign guests. In the twelve months beginning in October 1971, according to meticulous records maintained by Janet Irwin, then serving MacMaster as administrative assistant, there were visits by three hundred such notables—from Dr. Hemchandra Gupte, mayor of Bombay, India, and Egon Jensen, home secretary of Denmark, to Gabriel Gicogo of Kenya's Ministry of Home Affairs and Dr. Chen Chi-sen, chairman of the department of labor relations in the College of Chinese Culture in Seoul, Korea—while hundreds of others came in groups whose home countries ranged from Belgium to Israel. (The most recent annual representative six-day survey showed over fifty thousand visitors from twenty-eight hundred American cities and a thousand from 230 communities in fifty-eight foreign lands.)

Many of the individual visitors are invited to leisurely lunches in a private dining room in the tradition established by Lohr. More assiduously than his predecessor and mentor, MacMaster delights in bringing together at these special and even daily luncheons representatives of widely varying fields of endeavor, so that at one of them might be gathered a famous surgeon, a newspaper columnist, an insurance executive, a composer, and a government official, along with selected members of the Museum staff.

MacMaster especially enjoys taking distinguished foreign visitors through the Museum and explaining as well as the most experienced guide-lecturer the details of any one of the several hundred exhibits on the three floors. He never fails to note and be amused by the instant reactions of directors or officials from European museums who, accustomed to the almost funereal silence of their own institutions, are always startled by the rush of sound from hundreds and often thousands of voices—mostly those of children—echoing through the Museum. His years of experience have, of course, convinced him of the merits of the system that prevails at the Museum. "To have more freedom, to be allowed to speak, to be relaxed and natural and without being constantly told, either by signs or by attendants, to be silent—that is the essence of our democratic system," he likes to say. "Our noise level is undoubtedly the highest of that of any museum anywhere in the world. And that's fine!"

4.

MacMaster readily admits that it is not possible to measure with specific accuracy the lasting effects of a youngster's exposure to the multitude of scientific and industrial stimuli at the Museum and what influence they have in the shaping of lives and careers. Nor is there any really scientific way to measure what young visitors actually learn through this kind of informal education. Yet he frequently and ardently argues in support of his theories with adherents of formalized edu-

cation who maintain that learning must be achieved in sequential form and that pushing a button here or listening to
a recorded lecture there or spinning a dial elsewhere is
meaningless. "You must approach each individual where you
can take hold of him," MacMaster once told an interviewer.
"I was forced to listen to chamber music as a child so that I
wasted a lot of adult time hating it and avoiding it. I am just
now learning that chamber music, played regularly in concerts during the Spring and Fall months alongside the lagoon outside our central pavilion, does not have to give me a
headache."

Nor is MacMaster inclined to dig more deeply into ultimate effects by co-ordinating visits with classroom quizzes
or tests. "We really don't want to be associated with the idea
of the compulsory school, which is unattractive to many
boys and girls. We still do have school organized tours, of
course, but these are designed as informally as they can possibly be. And it is gratifying to know that it still holds true
that many of the students who first visit this place with
their class come back on their own and often bring their
parents or other young friends." Moreover, although opponents of his basic theories might not be impressed with the
fact, MacMaster has received thousands of letters from
teachers, parents, and, most happily, youngsters attesting to
their enjoyment and delight over having visited the Museum.
"We do not actively solicit such letters," MacMaster has frequently declared. "I myself rarely write a complimentary letter to a place I've visited and so I am doubly impressed with
the kind of spontaneous mail response we receive."

Two other well-established facts tend to persuade Mac
Master that whatever message the Museum has to offer is effective. One is that many of those who participate in the
Science Fairs readily admit that their interest in scientific
matters was considerably whetted by frequent visits to the
Museum when they were in lower elementary school grades.
The other is that as a place where students playing hookey

from formal classes in upper elementary and high schools are most likely to go, the Museum ranks as high as local movie houses and baseball parks—a distinction hardly shared by other museums or educational institutions, whether formal or informal.

5.

MacMaster's evangelism about the Museum and its primary purpose extends beyond statements to interviewers and special visitors. He enjoys lecturing and rarely rejects invitations to address audiences, whether they constitute the graduating class at a college in downstate Illinois or a New York conclave of advertising executives or the National Association of Photographic Manufacturers or the Deutsche-Unesco Kommission Conference in Essen, Germany. Invariably he espouses the Museum's cause, stressing its individualistic quality as an informal educator. He never fails to analyze and dissect the exhibit techniques of the Museum, originally devised in Lohr's earliest months and increasingly sharpened and improved in subsequent years. Delineating the standards set for prospective exhibitors and the rigorously detailed steps in their planning and preparation (in refurbishing a section of the vast "Motorama" exhibit in 1970, seventy-five separate architects' and designers' drawings had to be created), MacMaster always enumerates on such occasions the basic questions he and Harringer and Dr. Puffer ask themselves before any exhibit is undertaken: Can it be done? Will it communicate? Will it attract? If these can be answered affirmatively, further positive elements must be made part of each exhibit if it is to fulfill its purpose: telling a story in logical order by beginning with fundamentals and proceeding step by step to the desired conclusion, designing the exhibit so that it differs sharply from an adjoining exhibit and avoids monotonous sameness in the general area, providing visitor participation through novel devices, employing an articulate guide-lecturer who can hold visitors' attention and focus interest on the subject at hand, aiming the exhibit at the intelligent many instead of the highly educated few.

MacMaster's philosophy regarding industrial participation has not changed since Lohr devised it in the early 1940s. "What we do not want here ever is an advertising or promotional scheme. We get many proposals from companies who wish merely to display a new product, and that isn't what we want. Not long ago," he recalled for an interviewer, "somebody came to see me about putting on display a television set his company had made that is only two inches thick. That's a wonderful development and I'm happy to hear about it. But unless that company is prepared to tell a substantial story about how television works and its history, we cannot simply display this remarkable set. That would make of the Museum a kind of showroom, a trade fair. Industrial exhibits are not simple projects. We live with potential exhibitors for several years prior to the time an exhibit finally comes to pass. We work closely with officials of a company who have been designated to supervise the proposed exhibit and the experts hired to plan and build it. We confer, we plan, we exchange ideas, we sometimes disagree. Through all this, an exhibit comes into existence—not to remain static, but to change as conditions demand they change."

6.

Since MacMaster's assumption of the presidency, additions to the Museum's array of attractions have kept pace with preceding years while attendance has continued to stay above the three-million mark (3,159,892 in 1972). Among these has been a more complex microprojection system in the popular Microworld Theater, capable of such massive magnification of organisms undiscernible to the naked eye that an amoeba or a paramecium appears on a screen as formidable as a grizzly bear, alive and full of movement; a number of temporary displays relating to projects of the National Aeronautics and Space Administration, including moon rocks and the actual Apollo 8 space capsule —the first manned vehicle to orbit the moon—which had to be lowered into its space through a fifteen-foot opening cut in the Museum roof; and a new room in the "Motorama" area devoted to devices of the future, notably the Stirling engine, which works by external combustion and drastically reduces pollution. In addition, long-popular exhibits have been updated: Maytag's "Tale of a Tub," the Bell System's Hall of Communications, the International Harvester farm, and Union Carbide's Hall of Elements, where revolutionary applications of the astounding laser beam in metallurgy, surgery, and communications are displayed.

And of significance, too, is the result of a highly sustained campaign for new exhibits, so that more than $2,500,000 has been pledged by Peoples Gas Light & Coke Company, General Motors Corporation, Eli Lilly and Company, Sears Roebuck and Co., and other industrial giants for projects to be presented to the public.

In recent years, the Museum has become even more active in offering major temporary exhibits and innovative programs.

Typical of these in 1972–73 are the first comprehensive display of the engineering, architectural, and social-planning contributions of R. Buckminster Fuller and an exhibit of art works created through the use of scientific techniques by fellows of the Massachusetts Institute of Technology Center for Advanced Visual Studies, both made possible through matching grants from the National Endowment for the Arts, the federal agency created to support worthwhile museum programs; a two-part exhibition on urban and regional planning by Constantinos A. Doxiadis, the internationally recognized Greek architect and city planner; a second showing of the exhibits from the White House "Conference on the Industrial World Ahead: A Look at Business in 1990"; and a group of environmental projects, including a "Working for a Better Environment" puppet show and illustrated lectures and a series of science-oriented plays, presented jointly with the Art Institute's Goodman Memorial Theater.

To be of greater service to black and Spanish-speaking communities, special exhibits and cultural programs have been created. In co-operation with the Chicago *Daily Defender* and the Continental Illinois National Bank & Trust Company, an annual "Black Esthetics" art display and theater program was inaugurated. In 1972 the Museum set up Mexican-American and Puerto Rican advisory committees, published a bilingual guide to the Museum, and presented four exhibits and eight cultural programs of special interest to the more than six hundred thousand Latin Americans living in the Chicago area.

Many of these were devised by a newcomer, Dr. Victor J. Danilov, a vice-president since 1971. For years a journalist and educator, Danilov had been involved with science and technology at the Illinois Institute of Technology and the IIT Research Institute and as editor-publisher of *Industrial Research*, a technical news magazine for research scientists, engineers, and managers. For nearly a decade the publication had carried on a search for the one hundred most significant new technical products produced annually, a project that had added to Danilov's reputation as an authority on new-product development, technological entrepreneurship, and scientifically based economic development. These products have been displayed in the Museum since 1969. Initially Danilov had pondered whether he was "the museum type," but upon assuming his position he quickly found that his background blended closely with the institution's needs and challenges. Besides organizing the Fuller, MIT, and Doxiadis exhibitions and initiating the programs for Spanish-speaking people, Danilov served as chairman of conferences on metric change and industrial planning, sought out federal funds for Museum programs, conceived the environmental programs and science-oriented theater for children and an exhibit on the Great Lakes states, and immersed himself in a multitude of other Museum operations. In October 1972—shortly after the American Revolution Bicentennial Commission responded favorably to his proposal for a $350,000 exhibit on "America's Inventive Genius" in 1976—Danilov was appointed the Museum's director, with MacMaster continuing as president and chief executive officer.

7.

"We are constantly cognizant of the present," MacMaster is fond of saying, "but we are always aware of the exciting future and the incredible potential of that future."

And whenever he contemplates that future he reflects inevitably on the past and his own involvement with the Museum of Science and Industry as a medium reflecting man's scientific and industrial progress. "When I first joined the staff of the Museum of Science and Industry, every square inch of the building's 600,000 square feet of floor space had been allocated, presumably forevermore, by the curatorial staff in its consummate contemporary wisdom to subject matter in the fields of the physical sciences and applications in the fields of industry. The trouble was that this was before the transistor, solid state physics, the jet engine, nuclear energy, television, antibiotics, the electron microscope, radar, sonar, space exploration, manned or otherwise, the laser, computers, supersonic aircraft and so many other things which fill the Museum today.

"If all these came to pass in the last three or four decades —many in the last two—it is obvious that we are riding on an exponential, geometric progression curve.

"The Museum of Science and Industry has retained its life and vigor and interest for a vast public by moving with the times. I want to continue to do that—except that I and those who follow me will have to be sharply and constantly aware that the nature of our society and our population is changing, and in an accelerated way, at the same time that scientific and industrial advancements are being made. Fifty per cent of our people are twenty-five years old or younger, and these are people different from their predecessors in many ways. We have a widening gap here between young people with more and more education, and an utterly uneducated major portion of the population. And this gap is quite different from the one that used to obtain a couple of generations ago.

"The Museum of Science and Industry should and can serve both ends of this scale. Those who are the underprivileged and uneducated are not to be neglected. This institution must not become so sophisticated that it moves only with the intellectuals and the highly educated. It must continue to serve the masses, to be truly a people's museum, and yet be alert to all that is new and advanced. We can do it here both ways, as we have done for so long. We can advance with science and explain the advances both to our peers and to those who come to us for education and knowledge."

APPENDIX

As it marks its fortieth anniversary, the Museum of Science and Industry adheres to the original principle of a diversified membership on its highly supportive board of trustees. Numbered among them are industrialists from varied fields, scientists, college presidents, teachers, public officials, attorneys, bankers, historians, civic leaders, Nobel Prize winners. Since 1968, board chairman has been Edward C. Logelin, vice-president, United States Steel Corporation. Elected vice-chairman then was Dr. George W. Beadle, former president of the University of Chicago and Nobel Prize laureate in medicine and physiology, who served until he was named an honorary life trustee in 1971, when he was succeeded by Robert S. Ingersoll, chairman of the Borg-Warner Corporation. In turn, when Ingersoll was named United States ambassador to Japan in 1972, his successor was Robert W. Reneker, president of Swift and Company.

Charter trustees, appointed September 16, 1926, were William Rufus Abbott, Sewell L. Avery, Edward F. Carry, Rufus C. Dawes, Thomas E. Donnelley, John V. Farwell, Robert P. Lamont, Charles H. Markham, Charles Piez, Theodore W. Robinson, Julius Rosenwald, Joseph T. Ryerson, Col. Albert A. Sprague, Robert W. Stewart, Harold H. Swift, Charles H. Thorne, Frank O. Wetmore, and Leo F. Wormser.

In subsequent years, trustees and their dates of election were:

Earle H. Reynolds	December 10, 1930
Fred W. Sargent	December 10, 1930
George A. Ranney	September 5, 1930
Samuel Insull, Jr.	January 19, 1931
Lessing Rosenwald	June 13, 1932
Clarence W. Sills	June 13, 1932
Solomon A. Smith	August 29, 1932
Col. Frank C. Boggs	May 16, 1935
Dr. William A. Pusey	May 16, 1935
William Rosenwald	May 16, 1935
Major Lenox R. Lohr	June 28, 1935
Philip R. Clarke	June 6, 1938
LeRoy Woodland (ex-officio)	June 6, 1938
Robert J. Dunham (ex-officio)	June 6, 1938
Ralph Budd	June 3, 1940
Charles Y. Freeman	June 3, 1940
A. H. Mellinger	June 3, 1940
Gen. Robert E. Wood	June 3, 1940
Dr. James R. Angell	June 2, 1941
Dr. Arthur H. Compton	June 2, 1941
Edward J. Engel	June 2, 1941
Dr. Ludvig Hektoen	June 2, 1941
Nathan W. Levin	June 2, 1941
John Holmes	August 6, 1945
Dr. Robert E. Wilson	October 1, 1945
James H. Gately (ex-officio)	June 3, 1946
James S. Knowlson	July 1, 1946
William A. Patterson	July 1, 1946

Fred G. Gurley   May 6, 1947

John L. McCaffrey   December 6, 1948
James M. Barker   December 6, 1948

Willard L. King   May 2, 1949
James F. Oates, Jr.   May 2, 1949

Dr. J. Roscoe Miller   September 10, 1951

Kenneth F. Burgess   June 9, 1952

William V. Kahler   July 13, 1953

Dr. Lawrence A. Kimpton   February 13, 1956

Willis Gale   April 8, 1957

Wilson W. Lampert
  (ex-officio)   February 5, 1958
Leonard Spacek   October 1, 1958

Edward C. Logelin   February 4, 1959
Dr. John T. Rettaliata   April 1, 1959

Dr. Lowell T. Coggeshall   September 7, 1960
Porter M. Jarvis   December 7, 1960
Joseph L. Block   December 7, 1960

William F. Collins (ex-officio)   July 5, 1961

Remick McDowell   June 6, 1962
Harry O. Bercher   October 3, 1962
John D. deButts   December 5, 1962

Solomon B. Smith   February 6, 1963

David D. Henry   March 4, 1964
Albert Wilcox (ex-officio)   March 4, 1964
J. Harris Ward   August 5, 1964

Crowdus Baker   October 6, 1965

James W. Cook   April 6, 1966

Bennett Archambault	February 1, 1967
Dr. George W. Beadle	February 1, 1967
Robert S. Ingersoll	February 1, 1967
Donald S. Perkins	February 1, 1967
William L. McFetridge (ex-officio)	August 1, 1967
Daniel M. MacMaster	June 5, 1968
Daniel J. Shannon (ex-officio)	April 3, 1969
Dr. John Hope Franklin	August 6, 1969
Charles L. Brown	June 3, 1970
Harold F. Grumhaus	June 3, 1970
William B. Johnson	June 3, 1970
Joseph B. Lanterman	June 3, 1970
Gordon M. Metcalf	June 3, 1970
Robert W. Reneker	June 3, 1970
William J. Swezenski (ex-officio)	December 3, 1970
Dr. Herschel H. Cudd	June 2, 1971
Dr. Edward H. Levi	June 2, 1971
Edward E. Carlson	June 2, 1971
Mrs. Hope McCormick	June 8, 1972
Robert W. Galvin	June 8, 1972
Frederick G. Jaicks	June 8, 1972
Dr. John E. Corbally, Jr.	October 4, 1972

ACKNOWLEDGMENTS AND
BIBLIOGRAPHY

In my research for this narrative about the Museum of
Science and Industry, I drew heavily and frequently on the
recollections and knowledge of a number of persons affiliated with that institution. They included its present president, Daniel M. MacMaster; Willard L. King, for many
years its counsel and trustee; Martha S. McGrew, whose
memory of long affiliation with Lenox R. Lohr is as sharp
as her wit; Dr. Victor J. Danilov, its director; and such
experienced and valued Museum department heads and
aides present and past as Alice Connor, Janet Irwin, Ber-
nice M. Martin, Fred Ashley, Olaf C. Harringer, J. Bruce
Mitchell, Vernon L. Pietz, and Dr. Noble J. Puffer. J. Robert
Van Pelt, for years an important Museum executive and
several times its acting director, was especially helpful with
memoranda about events and personalities in the pre-Lohr
era.

I was given unlimited access to all Museum files, reports,
and other records, and Carl E. Dude, its business manager,
and Sterling Ruston, its registrar, were especially helpful in
making such materials available, as were Roger Lone, Elizabeth Kaufman, and Jane K. Doi in furnishing data from
the voluminous files of the Museum's public-relations de-

218   *Acknowledgments and Bibliography*

partment, and Mary Jacobsohn in supplying essential books and documents from the Museum library.

Important assistance and co-operation were given by Marilyn McCree and Virginia Stewart of the special collections division of the University of Illinois at Chicago Circle; Harold Teitelbaum, retired chief of the history section of the Chicago Public Library's reference department; William Sannwald, former librarian of the Chicago *Sun-Times* and the Chicago *Daily News;* Patrick Wilson, head of the Chicago *Tribune* reference library; A. G. Wykel, head librarian of Chicago *Today;* Ann Tsaryk of the New York *Times* reference department; Solomon Byron Smith, chairman of the executive committee of the Northern Trust Company, who made available yearbooks of the Commercial Club of Chicago; Mrs. Homer Hargrave; Michaela Williams, formerly of the Chicago *Daily News;* Edward C. Logelin, vice-president of United States Steel Corporation and chairman of the Museum's board of trustees; Emmett Dedmon, vice-president and editorial director of the newspaper division of Field Enterprises, Inc.; James Barker and Samuel Insull, Jr., trustees of the Museum of Science and Industry; Rick and Mark Kogan, for special research aid; and Shirlee De Santi, whose many skills contributed inestimably to the preparation of the manuscript.

Prime among dozens of books consulted were *A History of Chicago,* Volume III, by Bessie Louise Pierce (New York: Alfred A. Knopf, 1957); *Chicago,* especially the article by Waldemar Kaempffert, pp. 45–50 (Chicago: American Publishers Corporation, 1929); *Twenty Million Tons Under the Sea,* by Daniel V. Gallery (Chicago: Henry Regnery, 1956); *Bankers, Bones and Beetles,* by Geoffrey Hellman (New York: Doubleday, 1969); *Fair Management,* by Lenox R. Lohr (Chicago: Cuneo Press, 1952); *Museum Adventures,* by Herbert and Marjorie Katz (New York: Coward, McCann, 1969); *Photographic History of the World's Fair,* by James Wilson Pierce (Baltimore: R. H.

Woodward & Co., 1893); *The Industrial Museum,* by Charles R. Richards (New York: Macmillan, 1925); *The Sacred Grove,* by Dillon Ripley (New York: Simon & Schuster, 1969); *History of the World's Fair,* by Benjamin Cummings Truman (Philadelphia: C. R. Parish & Co., 1893); *Julius Rosenwald,* by M. R. Werner (New York and London: Harper & Brothers, 1939).

Among scores of magazines from whose articles was derived information dealing with the Museum and allied subjects are *Business Week* (February 5, 1930; January 4, 1936; and June 30, 1951); *Fortune* (February 1936 and May 1948); *Harper's Weekly* (scattered issues, April–September 1891); *The Nation* (scattered issues, August–October 1891); *Popular Mechanics* (April 1931 and May 1941); *Popular Science* (July 1931, November 1939, and June 1954); *Progress,* the monthly publication of the Museum of Science and Industry (all issues, 1949–72); *Science* (scattered issues, 1926–43); *Science Illustrated* (September 1948); *Scientific Monthly* (June and October 1929 and December 1947), and *Time* (scattered issues, 1938–72).

Herman Kogan

CHICAGO
1969–72

INDEX